Girls
that
Invest

Girls that Invest

Your guide to financial independence through shares and stocks

Simran Kaur

WILEY

First published in 2022 by John Wiley & Sons Australia, Ltd

42 McDougall St, Milton Qld 4064
Office also in Melbourne

Typeset in Plantin Std 10.5pt/16pt

© Girls That Invest Limited, 2022

The moral rights of the author have been asserted

ISBN: 978-1-119-89378-3

 A catalogue record for this
book is available from the
National Library of Australia

Cover design by Alissa Dinallo
Cover background and internal page opener images: ©Voin_Sveta/ Shutterstock
Internal design and figures by Chris Shorten/Wiley

Disclaimer

The material in this publication is of the nature of general comment only, and does not represent professional advice. It is not intended to provide specific guidance for particular circumstances and it should not be relied on as the basis for any decision to take action or not take action on any matter which it covers. Readers should obtain professional advice where appropriate, before making any such decision. To the maximum extent permitted by law, the author and publisher disclaim all responsibility and liability to any person, arising directly or indirectly from any person taking or not taking action based on the information in this publication. This publication may not contain the most up-to-date information.

SKY4379284A-7423-4970-B817-9A681273BCA2_092723

Contents

Acknowledgements

To my father, Pushpinder Singh, for teaching me the importance of education.

To my mother, Gurpreet Kaur, for teaching me the power of faith.

To my best friend, Sonya Gupthan, for teaching me to believe in myself.

About the author

Simran Kaur is a financial columnist, international TEDx speaker, and founder of *Girls That Invest*, the number-one global podcast aimed at increasing financial literacy for women and minorities everywhere.

Sim's powerful voice as an advocate and educator has resonated worldwide, with the *Girls That Invest* podcast featured across the globe by *Vogue* (India), Business Insider (US), ABC News (Australia), CTV (Canada), University of Oxford Women in Business, *Glamour* magazine, and many more. In her home country of New Zealand, she's appeared on Newshub, The Breakfast Show, The AM Show, 1 News TVNZ, The Spinoff, Radio New Zealand, and Māori TV, and she writes a regular stock market column for news provider Stuff.

As a speaker, Sim has been invited to share her advice for would-be women investors internationally, from a TEDx talk to events sponsored by government agencies, global corporations and universities.

Girls That Invest was founded on the principle that investing should be for everyone. It aims to break down the misconceptions, demystify the jargon, and offer a step-by-step pathway that women everywhere can follow to start growing their hard-earned money — because it's only through financial independence that women can be truly free to make their own choices and take charge of their lives.

Girls That Invest has now become an online phenomenon: through her podcast, investing master classes, and social media platforms like Instagram, Simran has created a vibrant, supportive online community where women can come together to learn and to share their experiences and ideas.

The lessons Sim herself has learned about how you can think about, live more confidently with, and grow your money are now shared in this book. In *Girls That Invest: Your Guide to Financial Independence through Shares and Stocks*, Simran will take you through the basics of why and how to start investing. More than that, she invites you to join the global Girls That Invest community — a place where you can join the conversation with other beginner investors, from all different backgrounds, who are ready to create a better, more secure future for themselves and their communities everywhere.

'If you educate a woman you educate a village'

The nine-year-old analyst and me

The world of investing wasn't one I grew up in. My first memory of the stock market took place on the school playground in my fourth year of primary school. A friend was telling me excitedly how she understood what those company charts on the news meant—you know, the ones with all the green arrows with numbers next to them. Her dad had explained to her how to read the stocks on the TV and she seemed pretty proud of herself.

'What is this "investing" thing?' I asked myself. I too had seen those tables with the dollar signs next to companies like Apple or the USD. I knew what Apple was, I knew what USD was, but nothing made intuitive sense.

That evening I went home eagerly waiting for the 6 o'clock news to arrive so I could ask my dad the same question. He tried his best to explain the ups and the downs and the trends, but I just didn't get it. Looking back, I don't think he quite understood it either. But when you're nine you don't think that way. You assume you're just not smart enough for it.

It's not for me.

I'm not good with numbers.

I'm just naturally bad at maths, I could never invest!

Or, my favourite,

Look at me, I'm no rich man in a suit, I don't belong here.

These were the thoughts I had about myself, about money and about the world for the next 15 years. I knew I was somewhat smart—at least in academia. But investing just didn't. Make. Sense. So it must just be me, right?

The next run-in I had with investing was in my first year of university. I was waiting in line to get into a lecture when a classmate told me about a student he knew who paid off his medical school loans through investing—while still at university. I was studying science at the time, and at that point I didn't even know what a supply and demand graph looked like.

'How'd he do it?' I asked, in awe of the possibility of graduating debt-free and how so much money could be made in the market.

'His dad works in finance,' my friend replied.

'Well my family doesn't work in finance, so I guess I'll never know how to invest' somehow seemed like the most logical thing to say at the time.

Let's unpack that for a moment: I didn't bother to open my mind to the possibility of asking more questions. If I didn't understand something, why didn't I ask? There are so many questions now that I would have asked:

Who was he?

How did he do it?

Could I talk to him?

Was this something I could learn?

Was there a book or resource his dad could recommend?

Instead, young Simran shut down the idea of investing before she even gave herself a chance to explore the concept further. She didn't believe she was capable of learning, so she didn't bother trying. That was my second run-in with investing, yet, despite being older than nine, my response was still the same:

It must be me. I'm just not smart enough to understand how to invest.

The world of investing has never really opened its arms to women or minorities. At best it's maybe looked over its shoulder at us and given a shrug. Or perhaps reluctantly invited us to the party hoping the invite would somehow get lost in the mail. Financial education has been scarce, and it has not been accessible. The jargon is full of heteronormative, classist and guilt-inducing language. No wonder no-one is listening.

It's a concept women and minorities around the world are all too familiar with. With a number of studies showing only 16 to 20 per cent of women invest, and with women only having 44 cents for every dollar of men's wealth (according to the US 2019 Survey of Consumer Finances, conducted by the Federal Reserve Board), we're lagging behind when it comes to financial wellness and growth.

We've all heard of the wage gap, where women who are in the same field with the same experience are making less than their male colleagues. But very little attention is given to the wealth gap. When we aren't making enough and aren't investing enough, we see a much larger, much more damaging financial gap with cis white men on one side and, quite frankly, everyone else on the other.

You may have assumed that women and minorities just aren't good with money, or we just aren't smart enough to handle it. The truth is our relationship with money goes much deeper. Centuries deeper. Despite what our inner voice has been telling us, it has less to do with us and more to do with the way the world has worked, up until now.

You might THINK you're bad at money because you don't feel you're 'naturally good with numbers' but maybe it's a result of:

- institutional and structural barriers

- money media not representing us

- a culture of shame around discussing money.

Let me break it down.

Institutional and structural barriers

A lot of us view our lack of financial literacy as a direct result of our own intelligence, much like I did in the past. I had the privilege of attending the best public schooling in my country, and yet the concepts of personal finance and investing were never introduced to us. The only financial education I had received up to that point was when representatives from a bank visited our school and handed out free piggy banks.

We're quick to blame ourselves for our lack of financial literacy and yet fail to recognise that we've had years of financial autonomy shaved off compared to our male counterparts. How can we compare our experience against that of people who have had a thousand-year head start? The financial industry was created for men, by men. The jargon, terminology and systems were, intentionally or not, created to serve people like themselves. Women weren't on the boards of directors when the modern banking and investment systems were created, nor were there any people of colour chiming in with their experiences to create a more inclusive, holistic system that would go on to benefit everyone who used it.

Women around the world weren't able to do even the most basic financial planning for most of modern history.

During the 1700s in the US and UK, British common law allowed for husbands to have complete control of any property a woman brought into the marriage. Progress was slow: in 1771 women were allowed to have a voice on how husbands managed their joint assets. How generous. Women weren't able to open up their own businesses either. In 1787, women in Massachusetts, US, were allowed to run their own businesses, but this was more about taking over for their husbands when the men had to go to sea. It wasn't quite a feminist act. It's also important to acknowledge that in the US these laws only applied to 'women of European descent', not all women—African American women were still without basic human rights during this time and were completely kept out of the financial sphere.

It wasn't till 1900, only 120 years ago, when women in every state in the US were able to control property. In Australia and New Zealand, it was 1884. In the UK, it wasn't until 1922, and in India, 1956. That's only one to three generations ago where the women in our families could control their own property.

Only in the 1960s and 1970s were women able to open up a bank account, get their own credit card or even get a mortgage.

Before the US *Equal Credit Opportunity Act* passed in 1974, single, widowed or divorced women in the US still had to bring in a man to co-sign credit applications. Women in Ireland could only own their own homes after 1976. Single women in New Zealand were being denied mortgages even as late as 1982, some being told they needed their father to co-sign. How can we expect to know how to invest when less than 50 years ago we couldn't even open up a bank account? Even to this day, women in certain parts of the world still struggle to access their full financial rights. While there are no laws in countries like Saudi Arabia prohibiting women from buying or renting property, there are many hurdles they must jump if they try to do this without an approving male guardian.

Until quite recently, buying property and investing in shares were not on the list of things women could do to generate wealth. They had to rely on their fathers, husbands and brothers to take care of their financial wellbeing. Inheritances were still largely given to the male child, and in some corners of the world these practices are still occurring.

We have missed out on thousands of years of financial discourse. Fathers passed this information down to their sons, but why tell your daughter the importance of investing or saving when she can't even open up a bank account alone?

Still, this doesn't mean women weren't smart with money. In many cultures, including the South Asian culture I grew up with, grandmothers and mothers would collect gold jewellery as a hedge against inflation — a concept investors now incorporate into their stock market investing strategies with gold. They would then pass it down to their daughters when they left their village for marriage. No bank account? No problem. Gold is a valued commodity, and one that can easily be liquidated for cash in case of an emergency.

You see, women always knew the value of money, always knew the importance of investing and always passed down their version of financial literacy to their children. Replace 'gold' with any heirloom, whether it be silver, copper, jewellery or cutlery, and you'll quickly realise this was happening in many cultures; women invested in the commodities available to them. Our grandmothers and great grandmothers knew the importance of being financially independent. We've always been good with investing, despite living in systems that were trying to keep us out. But now is the time for us to learn about the formal financial structures that used to be unavailable to us.

Money media not representing us

Mainstream media have done a great job at portraying the credit-card loving, shopaholic woman. Millennials and Gen Z in particular grew up watching these classics: Alicia Silverstone in *Clueless* portrayed a character completely out of touch with her finances, and clever Carrie Bradshaw in *Sex and the City* was still somehow not clever enough to afford a down payment on an apartment.

Why?

Due to buying too many shoes.

I watched *Confessions of a Shopaholic* as a child and vividly remember the scene where Rebecca, the protagonist, is so moved by a green scarf she sees in a shop window that she must have it, despite being debt-ridden. 'You just got a credit card bill of $900—you do not need a scarf,' Rebecca tells herself, but ultimately ends up splitting the payment across four different credit cards. I received the message that that was how I was meant to act.

The messaging didn't change as I grew older; in *The Wolf of Wall Street*, the two largest female roles in the 'financial movie of the decade' show that women either think money is evil and want no part of it like Jordan Belfort's first wife, Denise Lombardo, or are gold diggers who would leave a man if he lost his wealth like his second wife, Nadine Caridi. There is no in between. The only notable female trader in the office depicted in the movie agrees to have her head shaved in front of the trading floor for $10 000 so she can use the money to get D-cup breast implants. Let me make it very clear that cosmetic surgery itself is not the issue. But through the male gaze the movie depicted this woman, the one representative for women on the trading floor, as nothing but a frivolous spender. In reality, a female broker winning $10 000 would have likely considered investing the money.

Money media speak to men about growing their wealth and portray it as a masculine trait. Articles directed at men talk about investing strategies or encourage debates about the latest cryptocurrency, while articles directed at women tell us about a new hack to save $10 a week on groceries. And it's not just anecdotal: a 2018 analysis by Starling Bank in the UK scanned over 300 finance articles and showed 70 per cent of money media directed at men discussed investing, while 65 per cent of money media directed at women were about spending less. Women are told financial planning is complex, threatening and 'a minefield'. Men, on the other hand, are encouraged to speak about portfolios and take on risk, and themes of strength and power dominate. This encouragement of men to take on more risk and of women to be mindful and have a scarcity mindset is damaging to what young women expect their relationship with money to look like.

The visual content in articles about money pushes this narrative further. In 2021, social representation expert Professor Shireen Kanji at Brunel University audited image libraries to explore how women were being displayed. The results were not surprising: finance articles targeting women showed photos of women smiling next to a piggy bank, displaying a childlike concept of money. In fact, women were nearly four times as likely to be depicted like children compared to men. Yet men were shown in suits, making financial deals or having multiple screens in front of them. Men were more likely to be shown holding notes, while women were more likely to be pictured with pennies in their hands. In couple photos, which were largely of cisgender heterosexual white couples, women were shown to be watching as the man handled the finances. There was also an overall lack of diversity, again pushing the outdated, classist stereotypes surrounding money. These depictions really do matter; how we see people around us can negatively affect what we believe we are capable of.

I ran into this myself on a live TV interview. As I was speaking about breaking down the barriers to investing for women, the network chose to use images of men in suits and overcomplicated graphs as B roll visuals. I'm sure it wasn't intentional, but the irony of using those images to illustrate what I was speaking about was telling.

At a surface level, this may not seem like a big deal. But after years and years of consuming content that subtly tells you money is too hard to grasp, you start to believe that investing is complicated and only for men, while women are just inherently bad with money, or, worse, we're just not interested in our financial futures.

There is very little female representation within the world of investing itself. In 2016 in the US, only 11 per cent of decision-makers in venture capital were women, according to the 2016 NVCA Deloitte Human Capital Survey. Only 14 per cent of mutual fund managers globally are women, according to the 2021 Morningstar analysis of global fund managers. And in the US, only 31 per cent of financial advisers are women according to 2021 US Bureau of Labor statistics. That same study shows that in only 2 per cent of American households do mothers take the lead in investing, and the figures are just as bleak in other parts of the world.

Sallie Krawcheck and Cathie Wood, both upper-class white women, are the only female investment powerhouses that we have in a sea of Warren Buffetts, Charlie Mungers, Benjamin Grahams and Peter Lynches. Representation is powerful, and until we have more women and minorities in the mainstream showing us what investors can look like, we will continue raising another generation of young women who believe that they aren't capable of being good investors.

A culture of shame around discussing money

Money is still seen as a taboo subject, one even parents are uncomfortable speaking about with their children. We grow up being told you don't ask people about their age, religion, politics and *especially* not money.

For some odd reason I was stubbornly immune to these messages. I would always query my parents about our finances: how much did mum and dad make, how much did it cost for them to buy a home (back when home ownership was affordable), what was the cost of the car and why did they buy a cheaper old one in cash rather than a nicer car with a loan?

Whenever I visited the homes of friends who had money, I'd always ask what their parents did for a living so I could understand how they got to where they were. I have to admit I was a bit of a nosy kid, but to me the secrecy surrounding money never made sense. Knowledge is power. I would find those conversations both fascinating and helpful in growing my own money mindset—my relationship with how I viewed money—and understanding what steps other people took to get to where they were. Especially if I wanted to get there.

> *I truly believe keeping silent about money benefits no-one but those who are already powerful.*

By keeping silent about money we only make it harder for women and minorities to get paid more, to negotiate better, to learn how to invest; by keeping money as a taboo topic, we only make it harder for more people to understand how wealth creation works. Who's benefiting from our silence? Not us.

I love referring back to a panel that included Sallie Krawcheck, where they discussed the fact that in our culture 61 per cent of women would rather speak about their death than their money (according to the 2018 Age Wave and Merrill Lynch report, 'Women & Financial Wellness: Beyond the Bottom Line'). A woman in the audience disputed that claim. In response, Krawcheck asked her: 'Cremated or burial?'

'Cremated.'

Krawcheck then asked, 'What was your income in the last year?'

Silence.

When we create a narrative saying 'speaking about money is wrong' or 'wanting money is wrong', we prevent thousands of people who didn't grow up with financially savvy parents, teachers or relatives from accessing financial literacy. While I agree with the sentiment that schools should make financial literacy compulsory, teachers are already up to their necks in planning, organising and transmitting information in highly underfunded circumstances. Conversations about money shouldn't solely be the burden of the schooling system.

Instead, we should be encouraging conversations about money in our own circles and communities; there are so many benefits to speaking up. Knowing what your colleagues make can be used to make sure you're not falling victim to the wage gap. Knowing what your seniors or mentors make opens up the doors to understanding what the current ceiling looks like. Speaking about the process of buying a home, what a mortgage entails, the benefits of credit cards and even what the stock market is, aren't necessarily conversations you'd have over coffee with your relatives or even your best friends, yet they are crucial to breaking down these barriers of financial literacy.

Everything is unknown until we talk about it, and the only way to understand it is to open up the dialogue about money.

Money makes you ~~rich~~ free

I came to this realisation at a party. I was 13 years old, and my family and I were at a celebration for a wealthy family friend who had recently started a business. I didn't feel particularly money-minded then and, if anything, this uncle always seemed to be worried and busy. I associated money with evil and guilt—it was something that had to be taken off the backs of other people. On some level I believed that there was only so much money available, so for you to make money it had to be taken away from someone else. That would not be me. I didn't want to be considered 'money minded'. I personally wanted to spend my time enjoying my life, not chasing dollars and cents.

A woman I had never met came over and, in true 'aunty' fashion, asked me about my future and what I wanted to do with my life. I can't remember a lot of what she said in that conversation in between mentioning multiple times that her son was in medical school, but one thing did prick up my ears: she said I really needed to study hard, get a well-paying job and become financially independent. Because then, 'no matter what happens in your life, whether it be a bad job or a relationship, you can walk away and say no'.

I thought about that conversation a lot after the party. I hate to admit that, eventually, I forgot her name, I forgot what she looked like, what she was wearing and where the party was held, but I never forgot what she said. In order to have more control in my life, in order to have the freedom to live in alignment with my goals and values, and in order to be able to walk away from situations that did not serve me, I needed to be financially free.

I realised it wasn't wrong to care about or be 'focused on' money. Money affects every aspect of our lives. It affects our life expectancy, our health outcomes, our access to better resources. It affects our stress and mental health, our relationships with our families, partners and children. It affects our ability to enjoy our day-to-day activities, but, more importantly, it affects our freedom, our choices and what control we have over our lives.

It doesn't make sense for all of us to walk around pretending like we don't care about money.

The truth is, regardless of how you politically identify, in our capitalist society, money matters. Not for the finer things in life, but for the freedom it provides you. Sure, this book could be about how to overthrow the capitalism system, but we haven't figured that one out just yet.

If you work a job, pay taxes, pay rent or a mortgage, exchange your time for money and exchange your money for basic necessities like water, housing and goods, you are contributing to a thriving economy and (likely) a capitalist society. And if you're helping it grow, it's about time you took your rightful piece of the investing pie, instead of just letting the people up top reap the benefits of your labour. The money you earn from your investments can then be used to redistribute back into the causes you believe in, whether that be generational wealth for your family or the organisations and charities that matter to you most. We should not continue to be exploited and left behind due to a lack of financial education.

Money, most importantly, provides freedom. Too many times growing up I saw the effects of money being used against women. I came from a largely patriarchal background, and the financial imbalance between men and women is the foundation it stands on. I saw how the 'provider' of the family gets to call the shots. They get the final say. Too many times I saw women be asked to quit their jobs and become housewives, only to have their lack of income thrown back in their face during stressful periods.

I've seen women have their opinions not taken seriously because they aren't the breadwinner or don't have an impressive job title. I've seen women train for decades in their skillset, only to be pressured into giving up their careers to raise their children so their husbands could focus on their careers instead.

The patriarchy needs that financial imbalance to work. And the people who benefit from this know: many successful women in arranged marriages can tell you stories about how their education and job titles were used by their in-laws to show off how intelligent their future daughters-in-law were, but after marriage they were coerced by the family to quit working and perform household duties instead.

It doesn't take much searching to find women with stories of friends or relatives who have been financially ruined by a divorce or who've stayed in a bad relationship because of finances.

> *The only way to make sure we don't end up stuck in a situation that doesn't serve us is through being financially free.*

This was my biggest 'why' behind making sure I had the tools to be financially free. Like that aunty at the party, I wanted to be able to say no. Growing up with such strong ideologies around me, I never wanted to be in a situation where I couldn't leave because I didn't have the financial means to. Having an emergency fund and investments that bring you income when you can't work are vital tools for women—for anyone, really—to live their life on their own terms.

I like to call it f*** you money. Investing allows us to have f*** you money. Nothing compares to knowing that you 'got you' for the rest of your life, and that your life going forward will be on your own terms. Investing for yourself is investing in your own freedom and choices.

This book isn't going to teach you how to become rich quickly, but it will teach you how to grow wealth like generations of families have before us. It'll show you the strategies we were never taught, decode the language we never learned, and walk you step by step through how to grow a stock market portfolio like a professional, so that you can reap the rewards of financial independence and create generational wealth.

There are many concepts you'll find throughout this book where you'll realise it's not nearly as complicated as it's seemed. It's not 20 layers deep, with lots of intricacies and nuances that the average investor needs to know. One may never know everything when it comes to the stock market, as it is constantly evolving, but once you know enough through this book, you'll have the tools you need to get started.

Let's begin.

How to use this book

This book is a guide, or investing bible if you will, that is going to set out chapter by chapter the information you need to know to begin your investing journey. You may already have a bit of an idea or have dabbled in shares, or you may have no clue where to begin—either way, by the end of this book you'll have a clear idea of not only the foundational information of the investing world, but what to learn, what to unlearn and how to begin your journey.

Part I of the book breaks down the 'why' behind investing and the fundamentals that all investors should know. It's a critical step in making sure you feel confident and knowledgeable about your journey. It may seem tiresome to get through all this information before we get into the juicy parts of 'how' to invest, but it's important for your overall stock market knowledge set. Think of it as your theoretical learning.

Part II of this book then gets into the investing styles and strategies that you can use. Each chapter is a tool you can take away to form your hybrid investing method. One person's way of investing may not suit someone else, but it's important to know what is out there so you are empowered to make that decision. Think of it as your practical learning.

At the end of each chapter is a list of actionable steps to take, so that you get the most out of this book. Once you put the theory and practical knowledge together, you have a sound guide that you can refer back to.

Note: Please, write on this book, fold the corners of pages—you have my permission! Use highlighters, circle terms, fill up this book with coloured Post-it notes. This book is to be used, revisited and, most importantly, shared.

Part I
Why become an investor?

1

Five reasons investing is better than a mattress stuffed with cash

In our day-to-day jobs, we trade our time for our wage. But there's only 24 hours in a day, eight of which should go to sleep. To have wealth you need to make money, but to make more money you need to give up more time, and giving up more time means not being able to enjoy your money. It's a rat race no-one wants to be a part of.

This is where passive income comes in. Passive income is the money you earn without working, but no other passive income stream works the way investing does. And the best part is that it can work on autopilot.

You don't have to wake up at 6.30 am and sit through rush hour traffic for investing to work. You don't have to sit through a Zoom meeting that could have been an email for compound interest (which we'll get into in a later chapter) to do its thing. It's the definition of making your money work hard for you, rather than just working hard for your money. And, unlike time, it's scalable.

Before we learn how to invest, it's important to know why we should invest in the first place. It's not even related to having enough income first; my best friend Sonya Gupthan and I, through our *Girls That Invest* podcast, have come across countless successful women with their net worth in the six-figure range. They have their bills automated, their insurance covered, their savings growing and they are very well versed in every other aspect of their financial journey. They're the women who look like they've 'made it', and they rightfully have.

However, for some reason, when it comes to investing, they just haven't started and they don't know how to begin. It's a phenomenon we seem to come across no matter where in the world we meet these women.

The majority of us know we should be investing, but no-one teaches us how or why.

Understanding the 'why' behind investing is a powerful tool. When you have intention and place value on an action, you're more likely to commit to the goal and you're more likely to stick through the rougher moments.

When medical students go through their training, they aren't called university students for five years and then 'doctor' on year six. They're called student doctors. I lived in a flat with three friends in medical school who had just begun the clinical part of their degree, where they went from studying in lectures to being in hospitals. When they'd come home from their training days at the hospital, exhausted from dealing with condescending consultants, they'd feel defeated and even question if they were good enough — despite quite literally being medical students. Being called student doctors somehow helped lift up their spirits. I don't know why it worked, but it did. I think it was a way to make them feel like they belonged in a space where they maybe didn't feel like they were adequate.

So, before we go any further, from here onwards you get a new title: reader, you're a student investor, or, as I like to say, an investor in training.

An investor in training who knows why their money is invested and understands what they get out of it is less likely to panic when the stock market goes through a downturn. It makes sense, right? It's a bit like going to the gym for the first time: if you can see the benefits of sticking through to the end, you can get through the discomfort. Without this guidance, you'll throw in the towel a lot more quickly.

So besides the whole 'becoming wealthy' trope, why do people invest in the stock market? What's in it for them compared to starting a business or putting money away in a savings account? And, more importantly, what's in it for you, specifically?

Let me introduce you to the five key reasons why people invest in the stock market rather than stuffing their savings into their mattress:

- to beat inflation

- to take advantage of compounding interest

- to reach financial goals faster

- for financial freedom and security

- to help create a better world.

Let's get into it.

Beat inflation

In simple terms, inflation is where the price of goods and services slowly creep up year by year. Inflation is not your friend. She doesn't get to sit with us.

You don't notice the effects of inflation every single year, but you notice it when you get flashbacks about how those $4 ice creams only cost $0.99 in your childhood. Why on earth would shop owners do that? Well, it's not exactly up to them.

There are three main types of inflation:

1. **demand-pull inflation,** where prices rise because the demand for the ice cream exceeds how many ice creams can be made

2. **cost-push inflation,** when the cost of making the ice cream increases, and that cost is passed on to the consumer

3. **built-in inflation,** which doesn't have a whole lot to do with the ice creams and more to do with government involvement and greater economic conditions.

If you are somehow unbothered by the fact that your ice cream costs will increase every year, think about it this way. The problem with inflation is less to do with goods and services slowly becoming more costly, and more to do with the fact that the value of your dollar decreases annually. As time goes on, your dollar is worth less and less. One hundred dollars in 2000 has the buying power of $58.72 in 2022 due to inflation chipping away at it year by year.

Let's use another example: if you have $10 right now, you could probably buy two coffees, but in 2030, that $10 may go down to 1.5 coffees, and in 2040, $10 may just get you one. (Though mind you, after a flavour shot and a milk substitute, my current iced lattes sometimes creep close to $10 already.)

A millennial or Gen Z's favourite example of inflation is the cost of houses. We've all seen stories of how homes could be bought for as little as $20 000 in our grandparents' era, and now many of us live in cities where houses are unaffordable for most average wage earners, often creeping up to the million-dollar mark. It's something that isn't country-specific and is important to factor in, no matter where you live.

Inflation isn't new. It can be traced back to the sixteenth century, when silver and gold coins were widely used as currency. An excess of these precious metals would lead to inflation. Governments don't like inflation; inflation was not our friend back then, and it's not our friend now.

In the twenty-first century, inflation usually sits around the 2 per cent mark annually. This means the money you have sitting in your bank account drops in value by roughly 2 per cent every year. **Every. Single. Year.** It never fails to amaze me how little we were taught about inflation, and yet the loss of money affects so many people daily.

If your boss gives you a 2 per cent pay rise, but inflation that year is 2 per cent, you don't end up with any more purchasing power than before. However if you *don't* get a pay rise and inflation is 2 per cent, your salary is now worth 2 per cent less—in simple terms, if you didn't get a pay rise to match or beat inflation, you got a pay cut!

I had a friend at work many moons ago who once came up to me and whispered that she'd had a pay rise.

'How much?' I asked.

'$3000.'

'Zoe, that's less than inflation this year! You should consider going back and negotiating.'

She, unfortunately, didn't want to ruffle any feathers, so she left it. That year Zoe worked harder than ever yet made less than the year before.

So many of us grow up thinking like Zoe, my prior self included. We grow up being told about the importance of going to university, getting a good job and saving our money. We believe that the road to success involves being good savers and, once we have six figures in our bank account, to purchase a black 'I've made it' Range Rover. We get taught to play it safe and not 'gamble our money away'.

It's fair to say Zoe quit not too long after that. But getting a raise isn't the only issue. Where we keep our money is as well.

In fact, according to a 2015 BlackRock survey, women tend to leave 68 per cent of their wealth in savings accounts. That's 68 per cent of women's wealth being chipped away by inflation, every single year.

On top of this, the wage gap is doing a number on us—how are we meant to close the wealth gap when we're making less, and the money we are putting away is also shrinking? It almost feels like a never-ending cycle.

The wealthy understand inflation; they had the privilege of receiving financial education, and, as a result, they know the key to building generational wealth is not through aggressively saving, but rather investing. They put money for their children not in savings accounts, but in funds that invest their wealth. Eighteen years of inflation is not something they would wish on their child, and neither should we.

This is why you should invest. Investors in training understand that, instead of stashing their cash in their mattress or in a bank account where their interest rate is between 0.1 and 0.3 per cent, investing is a much more coherent way to beat inflation.

The stock market has returned 7 to 10 per cent annually, on average, over the last 40-plus years. This doesn't mean the stock market stays between 7 and 10 per cent each year; some years it's up 20 per cent and some years down 5 per cent, but it averages out to 7 to 10 per cent in the long run. The benefit of something going up 7 per cent when inflation is 2 per cent is that you get a 5 per cent advantage over inflation (as illustrated in figure 1.1).

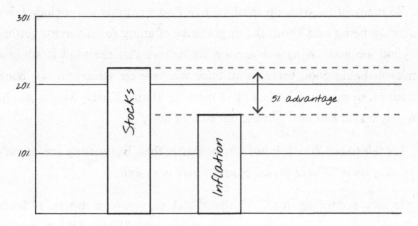

Figure 1.1: stock growth vs. inflation

By investing, you get to put your hard-earned money into something that helps outsmart inflation.

Take advantage of compounding interest

The story goes that there was a king who was shown a chessboard by an inventor. The king was so pleased by the chessboard he told the inventor he could have any reward he wanted.

The inventor pondered over this question, then responded with one simple request.

'Give me one grain of rice for the first square of the chessboard, two grains for the next square, four for the next, eight for the next and so on for all 64 squares, with each square having double the number of grains as the square before.'

The king was baffled—what was this inventor going to do with some grains of rice? He happily obliged, thinking he was getting a bargain.

The inventor came back a week later to collect his rice. But the king told him it couldn't be done. There wasn't enough rice to fulfil his request in the entire kingdom!

Based on the 64 squares, by starting with just one rice grain on square one, two grains on square two, four grains on square three and so forth, the king would have needed to have 18 446 744 073 709 551 615 grains of rice in total by the final square.

This is the power of compound interest.

Much like the king who couldn't visualise the effect of compounding one grain of rice 64 times, many of us can't always grasp the effect it can have on our wealth.

Compound interest is a beautiful thing where, when assuming a conservative 7 per cent annual return over time, your money approximately doubles in value every 10 years. When your investment returns money, we call this the rate of return (or annual return when you look at it after one year). Compound interest on your annual rate of return is the driving force that makes investing so powerful. Einstein even called it the eighth wonder of the world. And rightfully so.

So how does it work? Imagine that you have invested $1000 (this is your principal or initial amount of money invested), and you get 10 per cent interest on your money that year, giving you an extra $100. Great, you now have $1100 (this is your new balance).

Next year you also have a 10 per cent interest, but this time it doesn't just work on your original $1000, it now also works on your extra $100, so your money grows to $1210.

You begin to get interest on top of your interest, on top of your interest. And over time your money, like the rice, begins to experience exponential growth. Nice.

If the chessboard example didn't quite do it for you, let me show you with figure 1.2.

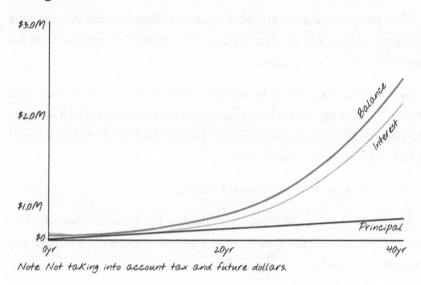

Note: Not taking into account tax and future dollars.

Figure 1.2: balance accumulation graph

Here's another example. If Devi puts away $600 a month in cash every year for 40 years, she'd have $288000. Not bad. If she kept it in a savings account offering 2 per cent interest she'd have $438866 — even better. But if she invested that money, assuming the stock market returned an average of 8 per cent annually (the market usually returns 7 to 10 per cent) for that same time period (ignoring inflation for all examples), she'd have made $1.94 million thanks to the compounding effect of the stock market. That's a $1.66 million difference in wealth for Devi, and it's too life-changing to ignore.

As with figure 1.2, you can see the value of having more years in the stock market. Due to compounding, the value of investing $1 in your twenties is more powerful than investing $10 in your forties.

And the thing is, you don't need a lot to start off with.

If Sarah started investing at 25 with even as little as $300 a month, assuming an annual rate of return of 8 per cent, by the time she was 65 she'd have $460000.

However, if Sarah decided she didn't want to invest until later on, waited until she was 35 and invested $300 a month until 65 with the same rate of return, she would only have $251000 — almost half of what she could have ended up with, had she started 10 years earlier.

If Sarah decided that she was going to invest once she had a higher salary and began when she was 40, putting in $600 per month — double what her 25-year-old self could afford — you'd assume that she would be able to catch up to 25-year-old Sarah's portfolio.

Surprisingly, 40-year-old Sarah would only end up with $359000 at 65. That's almost a $1000000 difference, despite investing double the monthly amount, and it highlights the importance of time in the market over investing with larger sums of money later in life. See table 1.1 (overleaf) for a summary of these numbers.

Table 1.1: Sarah's potential investment journeys

Age when starting to invest	Monthly investment	Total $ invested	Annual rate of return	Total at 65
25	$300	$114000	8	$460000
35	$300	$108000	8	$251000
40	$600	$180000	8	$359000

I do want to stress that this shouldn't discourage investors in training from beginning if they are starting off later in life. Not all of us had the privilege of receiving financial literacy at 20. Remember that not too long ago women couldn't get a credit card on our own—and for many of us, our parents weren't in the position to be passing down this knowledge. However, as the saying goes, the best time to plant a tree was 20 years ago, but the second best time is now. Whenever we have the opportunity, it's time to take action to invest towards our future.

Reach goals faster

Compared to any other way of seeing your money grow, investing allows you to earn a greater return. The time it would take you to make $1M if you saved $600 a month is 138 years. The time it would take to make $1M by investing $600 a month, assuming a rate of return of 8 per cent, is 32 years. People are shaving off more than 100 years by investing over saving—the difference is absolutely phenomenal, as shown in figure 1.3.

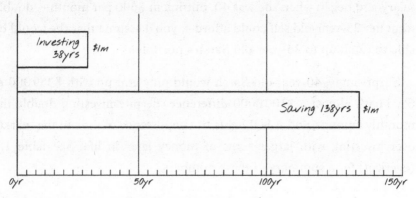

Figure 1.3: reach your goals 100 years faster

Through the power of compounding, investing helps you reach your financial goals faster.

Everyone, whether they think about it consciously or not, has some idea of what they would like their life to be like and the goals they want to eventually achieve, whether it be a dream car, or a home, or retiring early. For some people, their goals may include saving up for their children's education or growing generational wealth. We all have a certain vision of what 'living our best life' would look like.

To make those goals a reality we need to put a plan into place, and to reach these long-term goals we need to be able to fund them, whether that be with a term deposit, a high-interest savings account or any investment account.

The wealthy understand this concept well.

The average millionaire has over seven streams of income, and investing has always been one of them.

It just doesn't make sense for them to not be harnessing the power of investing to grow their wealth at a much faster rate.

Having goals that you're investing towards also helps to provide clarity, motivating you to be more mindful with your money. Investing can act as a savings plan. You'll start to have thoughts like: 'Rather than eating out twice a week, I can cut down to once a week, which is an extra $25 a week that I can add to the stock market, which alone would give future me an extra $150 000 in 30 years.'

Your brain starts to think about future you rather than just current you, and you begin to prioritise only spending money on things that bring you value, and investing the rest. I began to experience this myself with my investing journey: suddenly updating my earphones didn't seem like the best thing to do. Instead, I'd make do with my older model and put the $400 I was going to spend into the stock market. That's not to say we shouldn't enjoy the pleasure of the current moment, but your mind will start to shift when you being investing. I would liken it to wanting to eat more healthily once you start going to the gym. It just becomes an automatic switch.

The benefit of this is that not only are you investing, but you're also picking up good saving habits where it's no longer about your immediate needs. There's a bit of short-term pain involved, but it really does balance out in the long run.

For many investors in training, one of their biggest goals is having a strong nest egg for retirement. A 2021 survey from the US National Institute on Retirement Security found 60 per cent of women felt concerned that they wouldn't be able to achieve a financially secure retirement. Think about it: we work roughly until 65, yet the average female lifespan in the Western world is 81 to 85. That's almost 20 years of expenses to be covered. 20 years of rent, food, holidays, brunches, gifts for your family and the lavish lifestyle of your pets. It's going to add up.

While retirement can feel like a long way away for some of us, it's important to be aware of longevity risk. Longevity risk is the risk that your lifespan exceeds the expectation of how long you were going to live, and therefore results in you needing more income (or cash flow) to fund these extra years. Insurers and governments who promise pensions and elderly support take into account longevity risk, but it affects women directly as well.

In heterosexual relationships, women tend to outlive their male partners by an average of five years, and more often than not they are negatively surprised by what has been left for them in their family's estate planning. In fact, a 2018 UBS study found 98 per cent of widows and divorcees would tell other women to take a more active role in the money decisions at home. Having more of a say in money matters helps women understand and plan for their futures, and investing plays a huge part in this.

Governments already know investing is a powerful tool to help their citizens be comfortable during retirement. That's why so many countries have an opt-in retirement plan set up with employers, whether it be KiwiSaver in New Zealand, 401(k) in the US, Registered Retirement Savings Plans (RRSP) in Canada or superannuation in Australia. These schemes encourage everyday people to put aside a small portion of their pay cheque into an investment fund that aligns with their risk profiles and invests the money on their behalf. Many people assume these are 'saving schemes', but the money isn't saved in a bank account, but rather invested on your behalf.

It's also worth mentioning the shift in population demographics and what that means for you. Currently many OECD countries have a larger percentage of young people who are eligible to work, whose taxes pay for the elderly's government funding.

In simple terms, we have enough young people to pay for the pensions of all the elderly people. However, as life expectancy continues to grow and birth rates decline, we'll soon see a smaller proportion of young people having to fund a larger population of elderly (as illustrated in figure 1.4). This means the retirement age will likely be pushed past 65 and that there will be less money to go around to us when we're older.

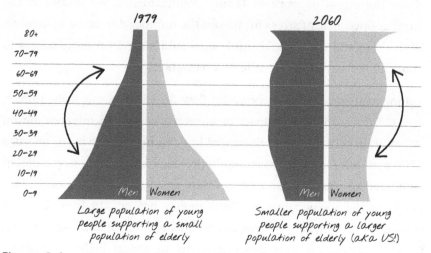

Figure 1.4: proportion of age groups in the population in 1979 vs. projected numbers in 2060

The next generation will eventually get fed up with funding our lives and will likely cut down or remove the pension system entirely. It's not a wild assumption, either: governments in the US, UK and NZ are already in talks about the possibility of reducing the support they provide our generation once we reach retirement age.

All the more reason to take responsibility for our own retirement planning and invest, and potentially reach those goals faster. Government schemes are helpful, but they often do not allow for withdrawals without reason until retirement age, and they often aren't large enough lump sums to live off entirely either. We are much better off if we have the means to stand on our own feet.

Get financial freedom and security

Money is a huge stressor in the lives of women—in fact, a 2019 survey by Salary Finance showed millennial women were more stressed about money than millennial men, and were more likely to suffer from panic attacks over financial issues. When it comes to stress, we often think about the stress of work or family commitments, yet money is the number one cause of stress for us and the number one cause of divorce. With those statistics, you'd think we would have a bit more access to financial literacy tools. Or at least a pamphlet.

Financial stability has a powerful flow-on effect in our lives. In fact, in 2022 the study 'The impact of a poverty reduction intervention on infant brain activity' found that providing mothers of newborns an extra $300 a month for a year ended up improving babies' brain development compared to those whose mothers were only given $20 a month. This points to the socioeconomic effects money has on our lives. Up to a certain level, money improves our wellbeing and physical and mental health outcomes; it improves our ability to access higher education, network into better paying jobs and frees up our time to connect with our communities.

A bird does not fear the branch beneath it breaking because it has faith in its wings. When you are financially independent and financially literate, you are more empowered and in a better position to make the calls in your life. No matter what life can throw at you, whether it's curveballs in your career or with the people around you, if you are financially secure, you will always have one less thing to worry about.

Nothing compares to the feeling of being completely self-reliant.

More importantly, investing helps to grow your wealth, giving women the freedom to leave any situation that does not serve them. Being financially independent means no strings attached. It means not having to listen to someone micromanage where you spend your money. Or putting up with a boss who makes you uncomfortable. It means not needing to stick it out in a career that drains you. No matter what the situation is, many women find extreme joy in investing for financial freedom.

Create a better world

Many people think money and creating social change are mutually exclusive, and that money is the root of all evil. This couldn't be further from the truth. You can pursue a financially free life and also only put your money into missions you support.

Ethical investing—investing only in ways that align with your values and morals—is a legitimate investing strategy (covered in more detail in chapter 8). While some investments include companies that engage in warfare, tobacco use and animal testing, over the past two decades there's been a shift towards ESG investing—investing in companies that place an emphasis on environmental, social and governance factors. In 2015, only $5 billion was invested into environmentally sustainable funds in the US, but by 2020 that increased to over $51 billion—and it's only growing stronger.

By being an investor, you can vote with your money. You can choose what types of companies deserve your hard-earned cash, and companies will take notice. Brands that promote plant-based meals or clean energy may be on your list, or perhaps you really want to back companies that have at least a 50 per cent female/male ratio in leadership—whatever causes are important to you, you can push for further change with investing. You can also vote by avoiding investing in certain companies based on their poor ESG ratings, or practices that you don't agree with.

If a large distribution company, for example, chooses to not let their workers unionise, or perhaps encourages them to stay in warehouses during a tornado, you can vote with your money by not investing in their company, or pulling out your investments, making it known that you don't support that kind of work environment and, for heaven's sake, to let people go home during natural disasters.

An example of investing for change was seen in April 2010. British Petroleum had a devastating oil spill in the Gulf of Mexico after their Deepwater Horizon drilling rig exploded. Piercing images showed the disgustingly vast amount of oil spreading across the ocean. Photos of the wildlife drenched in oil are scenes I will never forget. BP's shares dropped 51 per cent in 40 days on the New York Stock Exchange, losing almost $100 billion in value. Investors 'punished' the brand by pulling their money out, sending a clear message to BP and other oil companies that these kinds of mistakes would not be tolerated.

It's no surprise that millennial and Gen Z consumer spending is increasingly moving towards purchases that align with their values; thrifting, vegan products and recycled materials are shaping the way we shop and invest. According to a 2017 study from the Morgan Stanley Institute for Sustainable Investing, ethical investing is something 86 per cent of millennials are interested in, and 72 per cent of Gen Zs expressed hope that responsible investing could improve sustainability outcomes.

More and more of us are realising the impact we can have through our investing choices—after all, money talks.

***

Investors in training understand that there are many benefits to investing—it's not just about making money. It's about preserving wealth by avoiding inflation, making use of the power of compound interest, reaching your financial goals faster and, more importantly, being in control of your financial future. And it can also be about creating a better world.

Actionable steps

1. Research the inflation rate in your country this year—the value of your cash has gone down by this percentage.

2. Make sure your pay rise this year is in line or above inflation.

3. With a pen and paper, write down what you want your life to look like in five years' and 10 years' time. How much money would you need to achieve that goal?

4. Finish this sentence: Investing for financial security is important to me because _____.

5. Write down three causes you're passionate about. Research if there are any companies that align with your views, and how their stock prices have been performing.

Investor profile

NAME: Mireia

AGE: 22

JOB: Adviser at Te Puni Kōkiri (Ministry of Māori Development)

1. What does your investment portfolio look like?

It's 60 per cent ETFs (exchange-traded funds; S&P 500, NZ top 50, Smartshares Europe Fund, etc.), 30 per cent managed funds (Simplicity growth fund and Pathfinder managed funds), 10 per cent individual companies (Air New Zealand, Tesla, Apple).

2. When did you begin investing and what was your first investment?

My first investment was about $20 in Air New Zealand. I had no clue what I was doing and was only beginning to grasp the concept of investing. I remember thinking, 'When the borders open up then surely my money will increase in value?'

3. What stopped you from investing; were there any barriers you had to overcome?

Fear, anxiety and overwhelm around what to invest in. I tried to start investing back in 2020 after a friend had talked to me about the concept of it. I loved the idea of my money working for me, however, when I created an account on an investing platform, I felt completely lost and anxious around what to invest my money in! I remember comparing myself to all these people online who invested in companies before they grew immensely, and were now rolling in money! I remember realising that when I was looking through these companies, ETFs and index funds, it just made me feel afraid, because I didn't know how it all worked. I then decided to hold off until I knew what I was doing. The barrier I had to overcome was to educate myself and look at resources that simplified the concept of investing. I also had to not compare to other people's experiences, particularly on social media. At the end of the day, investing is a very simple concept that has been made complex.

4. Any tips for new investors?

Be clear on your intention and your 'why' behind investing. If I am investing for my future self and am putting my money in ETFs and managed funds that are diversified, then the market dips are simply a sale day! I am here for long-term investing that's going to grow my money over time, not for a short-term gain. Sticking to my intention helps me ride out the highs and lows of the market.

2

Misconceptions that hold us back from investing

It was a cold autumn day on 30 October 1928. Walter Thornton, a 25-year-old investor and model from New York City, parked his car, a yellow Chrysler Imperial 75 Roadster, at the side of a busy road.

He exited the vehicle and perched a cardboard sign on the windscreen. The car was worth a pretty penny at US$1555 (about US$25,000 today). The sign read:

$100 WILL BUY THIS CAR. MUST HAVE CASH. LOST ALL ON THE STOCK MARKET.

Walter stood next to the car and a small crowd of men in slacks, blazers and brimmed hats looked at his offer in pity. A nearby photographer snapped a photo of this moment in time. A photo that later became famous for commemorating this moment. What had gone wrong?

Source: © Science History Images / Alamy Stock Photo

Six days prior, on 24 October 1929, the US saw the Great Wall Street stock market crash, the largest crash the market had ever faced at the time. That day, later coined Black Tuesday, the entire market dropped 11 per cent. The crash signalled the beginning of the Great Depression, which affected not only the US but also all Western industrialised countries.

Many people view the iconic photograph of Walter, the man who 'lost all on the stock market', as a reminder of how risky the stock market is, using it to confirm that it's too scary and volatile to get into. After all, no-one wants to be desperate enough to put up their car for sale for a fraction of its price.

What many people don't realise is that eventually the market recovered, including Walter's losses. You see, in the stock market you don't actually 'lose' your money until you pull out your investments. If you have $10 000 in the market in 100 stocks and the market value of your portfolio dropped to $100, you still have those 100 stocks—they're just valued less until the market rises back up again.

That's what happened to our friend Walter. When the market began to rebound he recouped his losses and then some. In fact, he used his wealth to start a modelling agency only a year later. You see, you don't lose money in the stock market unless you sell your shares for less than what you paid for them—Walter must have held on and got the benefits of the rebound. His agency ended up being so successful it became one of the 'big three' modelling agencies in the US, notable for its World War II–era pin-up girls. No-one seems to remember that part of Walter's story. (As for why he had been so desperate for cash that he had to sell his car that day, that's been lost to history…)

There were other myths circulating around Black Tuesday, including the harrowing rumours that investors were jumping out of windows after seeing their losses and not wanting to face their families. However, research into suicide rates in the US proved no such thing—in fact, suicide rates were lower during that period. It was purely fear-mongering.

One of the biggest things that keeps investors in training from getting started is not their lack of knowledge, but the perpetuation of misinformation. And there sure is some misinformation out there. All it takes is one question about stocks at any family BBQ or work meeting to hear a range of false information about what the stock market is and why you should avoid it.

It seems like every Tom, Dick and Harry has an opinion on what it means to invest, and if you've been brave enough to ask the question, you've probably heard it all:

Investing is just gambling.

Investing is a con.

Only the rich make money, it's rigged.

Or my favourite,

My uncle's friend's son lost all his money in stocks; avoid it at all costs.

At face value, why would we question these statements? After all, if we don't know much about investing, we might be more likely to trust the opinions of those around us.

Unfortunately, many of these statements, though well meaning, come from the misunderstandings that surround the world of investing. No-one wants to see their family or friend lose money, so if they fear the stock market, of course they will very passionately tell you why you should stay away. However, it's important to be able to separate fact from myth.

An investor in training listens to these myths and chooses to do their own research to understand what to take on and what to avoid.

This chapter will break down the most common myths about the stock market so that you are well equipped to focus on how to invest, instead of wasting time worrying about what could go wrong. These myths are the following:

1. you'll lose all your money investing in the stock market

2. investing is like gambling

3. investing is complicated

4. you need a lot of money to get started

5. real estate investing is less risky.

Investors in training know that if you invest with the right strategy, it can be harder to 'lose it all'. Knowing the best and worst case scenarios puts an investor in training's mind at ease, and allows them to instead dedicate their time to doing what is important: setting up investments for the long term and being able to sleep easy at night knowing they're aligned with their values and goals.

Let's break down these myths.

Myth #1: You'll lose all your money investing in the stock market

This is the biggest stock market myth. If you've been scared off by it, you're not alone; even the most experienced investors wondered about this before they began, and it was a concern I had myself. After all, you work hard every day in your job or business — do you really want to risk losing all that hard-earned money?

You'd never light $100 on fire, so why risk it with the stock market?

Investors in training realise that people don't just throw their money into the stock market and cross their fingers hoping to make a gain. There are strategies, methods and hundreds of years of research that direct an investor's decision-making.

Firstly, there are different levels of risk in the stock market, and this can be both mitigated and matched up to someone's risk levels. (At the end of the book there is a quiz to work out your personal risk profile.) One investment can have a completely different risk profile to another; someone purchasing a Tesla stock would be after a much riskier investment, with the possibility of a higher reward, than another investor who purchases a Coca-Cola stock, a long-standing and stable brand, which, theoretically, encompasses less risk.

Secondly, it's important to discuss how people lose money in the stock market. The next time you hear someone recall how their friend of a friend lost all their fortune in the market, try asking them these three questions:

1. *What did they invest in?* Did they choose a few risky growth stocks after a 'hot tip' that these unheard-of companies were about to take off? Or did they invest in a broad market index fund that diversifies their risk across hundreds of companies and

sectors, so that if one sector dropped, another could rise and balance out their investment?

2. *What did they do when they saw their share portfolio drop?* Did they let their emotions take over and decide to panic-sell all their stocks into cash, thus solidifying their losses and not allowing their investments to gain back value once the market recovered? Or did they listen to the advice of their financial adviser and 'hold the course' and not sell their investments? During the GFC, many financial advisers had to beg their clients, even those who were to all intents and purposes intelligent and otherwise well adjusted, to not sell their positions during the dip. Still, many people sold. Those who held ended up not only recouping their money but making a great return in the years following.

3. *What do they have to say about the fact that the S&P 500, the index fund that encompasses the largest 500 companies in the US, has, since its inception, never had a crash that it didn't recover from?* If anyone left their money in a fund like that for a minimum of 15 years, so far in history, it was virtually impossible for them to have made a loss.

The questions are a bit harsh but they serve a purpose: to reduce misinformation as soon as it occurs.

The investor in training is aware that the main indexes (which is just a jargon word for 'list'—I'll explain them in more detail in chapter 5), like the top 200 companies in Australia (The Australian Securities Exchange 200, or ASX 200) or top 100 companies in London (The Financial Times Stock Exchange 100, or FTSE 100), have recovered from every crash they've endured.

In fact, let's go through all the major crashes in the history of the stock market to see exactly what investors mean when they say 'the market has always recovered'.

The market has always recovered? You heard me right; in fact, I'll share with you the graph that changed my life (figure 2.1).

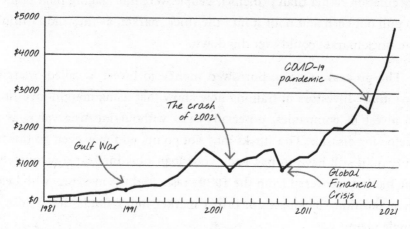

Figure 2.1: the last 40 years of the S&P 500
Source: Based on data from S&P 500 Index—90 Year Historical Chart. Macrotrends LLC.

This graph shows the movement of the US stock market; it's the S&P 500 index (made up of the top 500 companies in the US at any given time, also known as a broad market index fund) over the last 40 years. See how the market goes up and down in the short term but in the long term has a trend upwards? Despite every single crash, whether it be the global financial crisis or the more recent COVID-19 crash, the market has always bounced back.

Let's dive into the biggest crashes in history and what we learnt from the mistakes of others.

The 1929 Wall Street Crash

The crash in September to October 1929 was when our good friend Walter tried to sell his yellow car. On 24 October, the market dropped 11 per cent. At the time, it was the largest crash the US stock market had ever seen. Its effects shocked seasoned investors as it came after a period of a booming economy with great levels of production, and it led to what's now known as the Great Depression. Unfortunately, prior to the crash, the market in the mid to late 1920s was being driven by speculation rather than principle. People were mortgaging their homes to pull out cash and pour it into the stock market, as they didn't think the stock market could ever dip down.

The process of using borrowed money to invest is called 'margin investing'. Investors in training now know that using margin investing to invest in companies, especially ones without intrinsic value, is a recipe for disaster. The stocks may not go up, and may even go down, but you'll still have to pay back your loan plus interest. Fortunately, the market recovered from the 1929 crash, and the investors who held their positions in long-term broad market index funds didn't lose a single penny.

The 1987 Black Monday crash

Black Monday (or Black Tuesday in Australasia due to time zone differences) is known as the biggest crash in stock market history, even larger than the 1929 crash. It's widely assumed that the market fell due to computer-driven trading models that had made some errors. These computer systems were new to Wall Street and were basically tasked with engaging large-scale trading strategies. The market fell more than 20 per cent in two days. Let that sink in: the biggest two-day drop in the market was only 20 per cent. For someone investing in a broad market fund, at most, their stocks dropped 20 per cent suddenly. Not 100 per cent, not 80 per cent, not even 50 per cent. To date the biggest two-day drop of the market has only been 20 per cent.

Now you may be wondering how some people say they lost almost 90 per cent of their portfolio in this crash. Investors in training know that when someone says they lost a huge chunk of their portfolio, it was because they took on a greater risk to begin with by investing in individual stocks. The value of a single stock can rise and drop much more rapidly than the entire market. You can lose 90 per cent of a single company in a day, but it is very difficult for a broad market index to drop 90 per cent in a day—nothing like this has happened yet. Despite being the biggest crash, the market recovered only three years later in 1990. Meaning those who held their positions, again, didn't lose a single penny.

The 2001 Dotcom Bubble

It's probably equal parts morbid and nerdy to have a 'favourite' crash, but the Dotcom Bubble will always be my favourite. It was the perfect storm and a great example of what an investing bubble is: a market phenomenon where the price of certain stocks, industries or the entire market gets inflated much higher than what it's actually worth (like paying $100 for a $20 beauty blending sponge), until prices aren't sustainable and thus the bubble 'bursts'. It's like when you tell a little lie that keeps getting bigger and bigger until it all comes crashing down—everyone sees through your BS and walks away.

In the late 1990s and early 2000s, the internet was the 'next big thing' and internet companies were popping up everywhere. Any public company that had '.com' after their name began soaring: think pets.com or toys.com. Even if the company wasn't making a profit, enough speculators invested to artificially inflate its stock price. Because they thought they were going to make big bucks.

When the growth of investing into these empty companies wasn't sustainable, the market dropped. Those who had been trying to pick the next big thing were left burnt. However, again, the market fully recovered by late 2006, and those who were holding their positions in long-term broad market indexes didn't lose a single penny.

The 2008 Global Financial Crisis

You're probably familiar with the GFC. Even those who weren't directly involved or old enough to understand what was happening had a fair idea that 'the entire world was suddenly poorer'—and they weren't exactly wrong. In 2007, subprime mortgages (bad mortgages with high interest rates given to people with incomplete credit histories) were being handed out in the US like hot dogs on a street corner. People were even being *paid* to take up mortgages, a concept that leaves many millennials and Gen Zs today in disbelief.

Eventually, these dodgy mortgages started to catch up to people; homeowners weren't able to repay them anymore, defaulting on their loans and causing a large decline in housing prices. Lehman Brothers, a financial services firm that was in charge of a lot of these 'bad' mortgages, declared bankruptcy, putting Wall Street in big trouble. The stock market crashed, losing 46.13 per cent over the course of 18 months from October 2007 to March 2009, but recovered entirely in four years, by 2013. It then continued on a 10-year winning streak, up more than 250 per cent from 2009 to 2019. Again, those who were holding their positions in long-term broad market index funds didn't lose a single penny.

The 2020 COVID-19 crash

The most recent crash was the infamous COVID-19 drop in March 2020. When the world went into lockdown, the market momentarily dropped on 9 and 16 March. Investors in training know a crash is a buying opportunity, not a moment to panic. What we didn't know at the time was that the market was going to bounce back incredibly fast: 33 days, to be precise. That's almost half the length of Kim Kardashian's marriage to Kris Humphries. Most analysts predicted the crash would last much longer—after all, these were 'unprecedented times'. To everyone's surprise, the market went on to one of the fastest rises we've had in recent times. And again, those who held didn't lose a single penny.

***

Investors in training can see a clear pattern throughout history with every market drop. They aren't worried when the market becomes volatile in the short term because, if they are investing their money for the long term, the risk of losing money when investing in a broad market, low-cost fund is low. It's not impossible, but it's incredibly low.

Having this knowledge under your belt provides investors the confidence to ride through the ups and downs of the market.

Myth #2: Investing is like gambling

A lot of people worry that investing is like gambling. Let's role play for a second. Your name is Priya, you're in your best outfit and you're walking up the stairs to a shiny red carpet surrounded by bright flashing lights. It's not the Met Gala, but rather your local casino. You head over to a slot machine, the playful colours inviting you over. As you sit down, you hear the dings of the slot machines around you as players cash out. The sound is purposely engineered to arouse your senses and entice you to play.

You open up your wallet and put $500 into the machines. It's a lot of money, but you're willing to take a chance.

You're not just any ordinary gambler at the casino, though—you've done your research. You know the return on gambling is low. So low that you're aware the likelihood of making a return ranges from one in 5000 to one in 34 million.

After all, slot machines work with a random number generator inside every machine, cycling through millions of numbers and options.

You also know that in a casino, each time you play a game, the statistical probability is that you will not win. In fact, the more you play, the more the statistics work against you and the higher your chance of walking out of the casino with a loss.

Now, imagine you had a twin sister, Anu. Anu decides gambling in the casino isn't for her, and decides to look into stock market investing. She chooses to take $500 and invest in a Vanguard Total Stock Market Index Fund ETF (VTI), a fund (or basket) that is made up of every public company in the US. Anu now gets to own a small piece of everything from Apple to Zoom to some of the casinos themselves.

If Anu did this every month for 20 years starting from 2002, she would have likely made a 400-plus per cent return on her money.

If Priya returned to the slot machine with $500 a month every month for 20 years, the odds of her making anywhere near that return, let alone a positive return, is very slim.

Investing and gambling both involve risk, but that's where their similarities end. Gambling is a short-lived activity that involves chance, while investing involves choice.

When you're gambling your money, you don't control a lot of things. You can't research the dice beforehand, you can't read its company statements. You can't decide that the dice have a strong future outlook. It's all based on chance and speculation. And gamblers have fewer ways to mitigate risk compared to investors. If it comes down to odds, the odds are in your favour as an investor.

Investors are able to decide on their risk profile and invest in companies and funds that align with that profile. Investors are able to research their companies, see their past performances, understand their products, read their future forecasts and make decisions based on merit. Investors can read about the value of a company and decide if they wish to invest in them or not.

One of the most common misconceptions that lead people into thinking investing is like gambling is the misunderstanding of what investing is. Some people think it involves taking money, throwing it into a few companies and hoping for the best. That is what is called speculative investing: putting money into a company because you assume, or speculate, without any research, that the company will do well, or continue to do well based on past performance.

An example of this was the GameStop rally of 2021, which we discuss in more detail in chapter 9. Another example was the Tesla boom in 2021. Many investors saw Tesla ride upwards and couldn't see the stock dropping anytime soon. See figure 2.2.

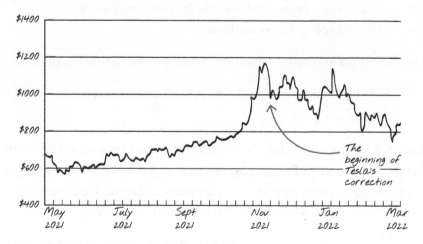

Figure 2.2: Tesla shares dropping
Source: Courtesy of Nasdaq

Unfortunately, as many investors of the time know, in November 2021 Tesla's shares finally began to fall into a correction.

A correction is when the prices of the stocks begin to fall because everyone wakes up and realises around the same time that they've been paying too much. Corrections are different to crashes, by the way. In a correction, prices only fall around 10 per cent. In a crash, prices fall more than 10 per cent.

On 9 November alone, Tesla stock fell 12 per cent. Investors in training who did their research would have noted the warning signs that Tesla was an overpriced share. You see, Tesla shares were forming what is called a speculative bubble. This is when shares are being bought not because they're a good choice, but rather driven by greed and the assumption that the price of those shares 'will never drop'. Clearly they hadn't taken on Bieber's advice to 'never say never'.

Four warning signs of a speculative bubble:

1. new investors who are not interested in the commodity but rather the short-term price gains

2. rapidly rising prices that don't reflect the company's performance or future outlook

3. lower interest rates, which encourages more borrowing to invest

4. increased media attention, which then attracts even more investors.

Speculative investing is not the way most investors create good investing habits; the majority of long-term investors prefer to keep speculating to a minimum and instead invest in companies and funds that they believe in, that they've researched and that align with their views.

Investing is all about intentional choices, while gambling is all about chance.

Myth #3: Investing is complicated

When I studied financial markets, I still remember gritting my teeth through my first lecture—reminding myself again and again that I just needed to believe in my ability to learn and understand the content. By the end, I was almost angry at how simple investing actually was, and how many years I had wasted thinking investing was too hard for the everyday person.

The truth is,

thinking that investing is too hard is a popular myth that holds most of us back from getting started.

We think that there must be some complicated process that goes on behind investing and that, because it is an activity primarily dominated by rich white men, with almost 90 per cent of fund managers in the US being male according to a 2021 Citywire Alpha Female report, it must somehow require more intellect or skill than the average person has.

I'm not sure who decided that if a white male does something, it must automatically be more complex compared with the jobs that women traditionally do. I think part of the issue is that representation does, in fact, matter. Famous female investors are few and far between: Sallie Krawcheck, hailed as 'one of the last honest brokers', is one of the few investors who made it to the front page of the *Wall Street Journal*, and even then she was only there because of her public firing.

The investing industry did a really great job at perpetuating this myth for as long as they possibly could. After all, fund managers make a lot of money when someone thinks it's all too complicated and would rather pay the fund manager a cut of their entire investing portfolio. Gatekeeping investing keeps certain people in business.

Now, I do want to note that there is a time and place for professionals in all areas. In some circumstances, it makes sense to hire a fund manager to invest for you, for example, if you inherit a large sum of money after a death in the family and aren't emotionally in the right frame of mind to invest yourself, or if you would like a hand to hold during the ups and downs of the market. Sometimes people with ADHD or other neurodivergent tendencies would benefit from having an adviser who provides assistance as required. There is no one right or wrong way to invest, but this book will teach you how to determine the best way for you.

You don't need a degree in finance to invest for yourself. The skills needed to invest are so simple once they are broken down. To this day, I've never met a person who couldn't understand how to invest in the stock market once it was explained in a way that made sense to them.

The Girls That Invest community is made up of women, men and nonbinary folk whose education levels range from those who didn't complete high school, to those with doctorate degrees. We even have people telling us that their bachelor's degree in economics or accounting hadn't even explained investing clearly. Due to their lecturers knowing the subject so well, it was almost difficult for them to articulate it in a way a beginner could grasp.

Let me set the record straight, investing does not involve many graphs and hours of following trends. It doesn't involve large risks and calculations. To buy a stock you no longer have to call up a broker and hear them pressure you into investing in the next hot thing. Thanks to recent technology, investing in a company or fund is as simple as going to an online store and buying a top. But rather than clicking on a Nike shirt, you click on the Nike company and take it to the checkout. And just like that, you become an investor.

Investing may not be complicated, but the jargon is...

There's no doubt the jargon is a huge barrier to entry. It's almost like another language. There are so many unnecessary words that prevent us from learning about investing on our own.

For example, if the prices of stocks are collectively rising, investors will say 'there's a bull market'. Or if stock prices are falling, they'll say there's a 'bear market'. Instead of saying 'What companies make up the bulk of your investments?' they ask 'What positions are you primarily holding?' As mentioned earlier in this chapter, 'margin investing' is when people invest in stocks with borrowed money.

Or my favourite, rather than saying Apple's stock price has gone down by 0.5 per cent, they'll say 'Apple dropped 50 points'.

'What on earth does 50 points mean?' was the first thing that came to my mind when I was learning how to invest. I thought it would make sense to break it down for you too.

The points system is a way for investors to understand how a stock is performing: is it going up or down in value? 100 base points is equal to one per cent, so if Google moves up 100 points, it just means the Google stock is up by 1 per cent. Or if Meta moved down 500 points, it's down 5 per cent. Rather than speaking about the movement of a company in points, percentages are much more intuitive. 'But that would mean people can understand investing, we don't want that!' said some financial rule maker, at some point in history. I assume.

You may be thinking, 'Alright, so it's not difficult to grasp investing concepts, but what about the maths?'

Luckily for us times have changed and the calculations needed for investing are becoming easier and easier to find online. Investing education websites such as Yahoo Finance provide investors with resources so they no longer need to whip out their old graphing calculator to work out the numbers. In fact:

if there's an investing ratio or number you need to know, there's already an online calculator for it.

The calculations of investing aren't difficult to grasp, either. In chapter 7, I break down the only investing ratios and numbers you need to worry about, so you can safely ignore the rest of the noise and focus on what matters. You'll see what I mean. And then you'll get angry for every instance someone made you feel like you couldn't invest because you weren't 'good with numbers'.

Myth #4: You need a lot of money to get started

A woman once shared with me the story of how she approached a friend's father when she wanted to begin her investing journey. She was a young woman of colour, in her twenties, and eager to learn.

He simply told her if she didn't have a spare $10000 it wasn't the industry for her, and she listened. As shocking as that comment is, it's a common misconception thrown around even to this day.

I used to believe this myself. In fact, I used to think investing was something I would learn about after I had a big house and boat; once I had a Kardashian-sized mansion in Calabasas I'd look into what a share is. As a child, I thought investing was what people did with their money once they had already made it, and it was just a fancy place to store all of their excess wealth. (I also thought an investing portfolio was a clear file filled with pictures of people's investments and properties, but I think I may have been the only one.)

My fatal mistake was to think investing is what people *did* with their wealth, instead of realising investing is how people *grow* wealth in the first place. Through the effects of compound interest, you are much better off investing with what you have now than waiting until you have the luxuries in life. As discussed in chapter 1, your money works harder for you when you invest $1 in your twenties than $10 in your forties. It is, however, important to speak about context: if someone is barely able to afford their basic needs, then those needs should come before investing. But if you have a spare $50 at the end of the month that you don't need for the next three to five years, then it's not 'meaningless' to consider investing it.

Now, you would be forgiven for thinking you need $10000 in order to invest. Not too long ago, to begin your investing journey, you really only had access to mutual funds—a pool of investments, such as shares of different companies, held in a basket—where the minimum to invest ranged from $1000 to $10000. Fund managers made money through percentages of their clients' portfolios, so in their defence it made sense for them to take on clients with larger pools of money. Think about it: would you rather work with five people with $50000 each or 500 people with $500 each? Fair enough.

However, now there is this beautiful thing called fractional shares. Fractional shares allows you to buy a per cent of a share. If an Alphabet share (Google's parent company) was $1000, you don't have to wait to save up $1000 to buy one share. You can put in $10 and get 1 per cent of a Google share. Now, technically even $1 is enough to allow people to become investors in any company!

You may be wondering how on earth 1 per cent of a share is going to help you achieve financial freedom, but the benefit of owning even a fractional share is that your money goes up and down the same percentage that the entire share would.

For example, if Google retuned 20 per cent in a year, someone owning $1000 worth of Google would get a 20 per cent return on their money, but so would someone owning only $10 worth of Google stocks. You don't have to wait to save up to be 'in the market' and have your money beginning to work for you.

The barrier to entry has never been lower. Investing is no longer just for the few rich and wealthy individuals who have a spare $10 000. Anyone can now have the chance to grow their investing portfolio, become an investor and create wealth for themselves in a way that doesn't rely on them exchanging time for money.

Myth #5: Real estate investing is less risky

Imagine if you had a pushy real estate agent called Mrs Housing. Mrs Housing comes to your home every day to announce how much the price of your home has changed in the last 24 hours. Today it's worth $500 000, tomorrow it's worth $490 000, meaning you've lost $10 000. The day after it's worth $15 000 less. The next day it's worth $10 000 more after the Manns next door sold their home for a higher price, bringing up the value of your home.

On a rainy day your gutter overfills and Mrs Housing lets you know you just lost $4000 in home value. On a day when you finally decide to weed your garden Mrs Housing pops by to say the value of the house just increased slightly: $500, to be exact.

Mrs Housing is a Type A personality so she tracks these movements every day on a spreadsheet and shows you a graph of how your house price is moving. She brings this graph every day, and you see just how volatile the housing market can be.

Many people perceive real estate investing to be less risky than stock market investing, but it's only because they don't have Mrs Housing updating the price of their assets daily. Homeowners would consider their housing assets a lot more volatile if they saw these daily movements. Instead, homeowners only really note their house prices a couple of times: when they're about to buy their home, when they remortgage it and when they're about to sell it. The average time between buying and selling your home is usually 7.4 years. If a stock market investor in a broad market index also only checked their index fund every 7.4 years, they wouldn't consider the stock market to be as risky.

Unfortunately, in the stock market this data is updated every second.

For example, take a look at figure 2.3. To the average person this may confirm their concerns that the stock market is too volatile. It's a graph of the Vanguard S&P 500 exchange-traded fund (ETF VOO), made up of the top 500 companies in the US, displaying its movement over the course of a day.

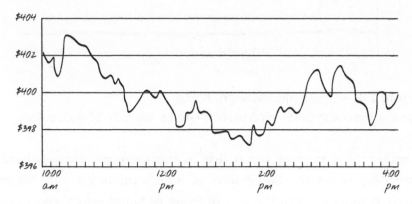

Figure 2.3: a day with the ETF VOO
Source: Used with permission of NYSE Group, Inc. © NYSE Group, Inc.

The highs and lows on this graph appear scary, yet all it's showing is that if you had one stock of this ETF in the morning it was worth $403 and by the afternoon it was worth $397—losing a mere $5, or 1.2 per cent in value. Investors in training know the important of reading the scale when reviewing the performance of shares. It can be the difference between something looking very volatile versus something looking flat, depending on the scale of the Y axis (the vertical axis), as shown in figure 2.4 (overleaf).

Home ownership isn't all roses either. There are also risks that come with it, unlike stocks that can be liquidated quickly into cash if you need it, when it comes to real estate investing you don't get the cash in your wallet until you have sold your asset, which can mean waiting weeks, months or in some cases even years (especially in the luxury market), which is a risk in itself. You also have the risk of property damage, bad tenants or poor weather events. People could even egg your investment.

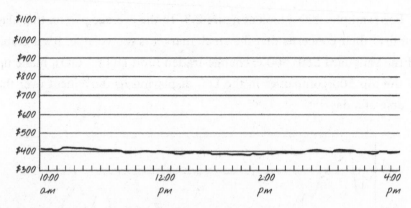

Figure 2.4: same data, different scale
Source: Used with permission of NYSE Group, Inc. © NYSE Group, Inc.

Another thing to point out is that in this economic climate, home ownership is not the easiest form of investment to get into. Wages aren't keeping up with the cost of living or house prices, and many young people are finding themselves pushed out of the market, but still wanting long-term wealth generators. I had a very similar experience: I couldn't afford a home just by saving, so I chose to invest through the stock market, which eventually helped me to get into my first home. If you don't have parental help (I didn't), investing in the stock market can sometimes be an option to work toward property ownership in the long term.

While property isn't a less risky investment, some may prefer property as it's an asset that they can see and touch, and therefore feels more real and grounded. Some investors find that owning a home can be a good investment as you can do up the place to add value, and you're more in control of the asset as you can decide on rent, who your tenants are and any changes you want to make. One of the biggest benefits of property investing is that you can also use it as leverage: you're borrowing money from the bank via a mortgage, but the increases in the property price of your home you get to keep. The truth is the stock market often outperforms how fast property prices rise, but that thing called leverage is why many people look into property.

Real estate is not a bad form of investing, but it's not the most accessible form of investing for the average investor. The risks involved in real estate and stock market investing vary, but in the same way that you can purchase bad stocks and lose out, you can also do so with bad homes.

***

There are many myths that surround stock market investing, and I'm never upset at any of them. It's human nature to protect ourselves from the unknown, and in this context that protection can look like statements that suggest investing is like gambling, or that it's too risky. The truth is that once the information is laid out clearly it's very easy to cut through the noise and realise investing is an accessible and frankly wonderful wealth generator for investors in training to use.

Actionable steps

1. If someone has told you that they lost a lot of money on the stock market, ask if they could explain further so you can learn what led to it.

2. Circle the investing myths you used to believe. How many of them did you have out of 5?

3. If real estate and the stock market had similar levels of risk, would you prefer one over the other?

Investor profile

NAME: Charlie

AGE: 25

JOB: Junior doctor

1. What does your investment portfolio look like?

I have a 20 per cent Simplicity growth fund; 30 per cent Simplicity balanced fund; 15 per cent Vanguard index fund; 5 per cent NZX 50; 20 per cent Mercury Energy shares (this was a gift from a family member many years ago); 10 per cent USA shares (even split between NVDIA, Apple, Tesla); less than 1 per cent crypto.

2. When did you begin investing and what was your first investment?

In 2020 with $2000 in the Vanguard International Shares Index Fund on InvestNow.

I spent many months researching and educating myself (mostly through the subreddit /PersonalFinanceNZ, and the *Girls That Invest* podcast, of course) and finally decided on this particular index fund.

I'm a hypochondriac but also super indecisive, which wasn't a good combination as I kept delaying making my first investment. I finally realised the best investing style for myself would be 'set and forget', so now I just make regular auto-investments into a couple of index funds/ETFs that resonate with my investing principles.

3. What stopped you from investing; were there any barriers you had to overcome?

Lack of knowledge and unsure where or how to start the journey, stigma from immigrant parents who had a negative view that investing was centred around a 'volatile stock market', which resulted in my own hesitation to invest, and being a student and not having any actual steady income to invest.

4. Any tips for new investors?

Time in the market is better than timing the market.

3

The first 5 bricks

I was 11 years old when I tried to make my first pavlova (a meringue-based dessert that's iconic in New Zealand and Australia). It's considered an easy dessert to make: you just need five ingredients, and the recipe I used suggested only 1 out of 5 stars for difficulty.

Surely, I could do this.

Part of the recipe included separating the egg whites from the egg yolks. I must admit I've never been the most meticulous person—I'm okay with letting a few things slide—so I separated the egg whites without putting much attention into it, not really caring that there were traces of yolk in the whites. After all, what's a few drops of the wrong ingredient going to do?

I was so excited to finally pull my crispy white pavlova out of the oven, and instead was dismayed to see a gooey yellow mixture that had bubbled out of the cake tin and onto the floor of the oven. I was both hungry and heartbroken. I didn't initially understand how it could all have gone so wrong. After all, it was just egg yolk! How could it affect the baking like this?

I was so scared by my mistake I never made pavlova again. That moment taught me a valuable lesson. Even for the simplest tasks, carelessness and a lack of preparation can turn your work into custard.

Or in my case, something that resembled custard.

The world of investing is no different, but let's switch metaphors here. It's important to have our foundations of personal finance established before we begin our journey to wealth. Then, brick by brick, we build on what ends up becoming the foundation of generational wealth that we and our future generations can reap the rewards from and build on further.

I'll be the first to admit that, in a world where everything can feel instantaneous, growing wealth slowly can sound painful. It's like wanting to start a sprint now but knowing you need to first hit the gym and build up your cardio. The excited part of you wants the results now, but the wise part of you knows you need to get the foundations sorted first.

Laying your financial foundations: the first 5 bricks

Before we begin investing, there are five personal finance concepts to tackle (the bricks in your foundation—see figure 3.1) so that you begin on the right foot. It's an important part of your overall financial wellness and you'll be thankful that you had this part sorted out before you bought your very first stock or fund. So, to lay your financial foundations, you should:

1. know what's coming in and going out

2. tackle high-interest debt

3. automate your money

4. make a rainy day fund

5. sort out your retirement account.

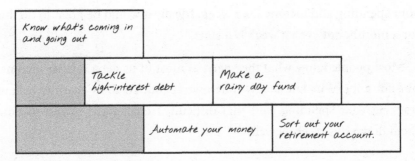

Figure 3.1: the 5 bricks

Brick #1: Know what's coming in and going out

The first thing to do before you begin your investing journey is to have a very clear understanding of how much money is coming in and out of your life. Some people call it checking your cash flow, or budgeting. Either way it's important to be crystal clear about your money. One of the most common habits of financially successful people is tracking their personal finance and understanding exactly how much they spend and make in a week.

Why? Well, if you can't track something you can't improve on it. Investors in training know it's hard to work out if we're getting better or worse with our money if we don't have metrics to compare it to. It doesn't mean tracking everything on a four-tab Excel spreadsheet, but it does mean knowing exactly how much you make and spend monthly. If I asked you what those two numbers were, would you be able to tell me?

I could suggest printing out your bank statement for last month and highlighting in one colour all the income that's come through, and then in another colour highlighting all your expenses, but that's painful. No-one wants to do that.

Instead, I recommend doing this: get an app that tracks your spending, or even just a notebook where you can jot things down and take note of your spending and income for a week. Ideally it would be great to do this for a month, but even a week is a start.

Most people know what they earn as most of us get a regular income, but not a lot of us know how much we spend. To show that the task of tracking your spending isn't that difficult, I challenged myself to note them down this week as well.

MONDAY: -$28 gym membership

TUESDAY: -$80 groceries

WEDNESDAY: -$25 lunch for me and my brother, -$7 oat milk dirty chai (highly recommended coffee order by the way)

THURSDAY: -$117.81 full tank of petrol

FRIDAY: -$7.99 a novel, -$470 my mortgage

SATURDAY: $0

SUNDAY: -$24.50 Gong Cha for me and Sonya

By knowing exactly what is coming in and going out, you get a better idea of what you can do with your money. For example, you may realise you spend a lot of money on things you don't actually enjoy. You may even realise that you're paying for a monthly subscription that you forgot to cancel. By knowing your cash flow, you can then get a better idea of how much you are able to cut out and rearrange, and therefore what you're left with to save and invest.

I find this to be a much better approach to money than trying to work out how much is left at the end of the week and investing that. It's so much more powerful to say that you have a set percentage per month that you put away into your investing portfolio. This gives you a much clearer idea of what you can invest after you account for everything else.

Value-based spending

Another benefit of doing this at the start is it encourages what we call value-based spending. It's like a budget, but rather than focusing on what you can't spend and cutting everything down to the bare bones, you get to allocate money towards the things that are important to you. This could be $300 towards skincare every year or $1000 towards travel. I've never been a fan of cutting down spending to the point where you cannot even enjoy the simple pleasures of a $5 latte.

With value-based spending you get to allocate your money towards the two or three things that are important to you and forget the rest. For you, that might be holiday travel or getting manicures. For someone else it might be splurging on higher quality clothing that makes them feel good. The point is that there is no guilt or shame associated with spending money, and instead you're empowered by spending money in alignment with your goals and values.

This form of cash flow management is also something that you're more likely to stick to in the long term. At the end of the day, it's better to be spending in a way that is aligned with your values instead of trying to stick with a harsh budget and giving up every few days. It's not about trying to deprive yourself of the few sparks of joy you get throughout the week; it's about finding a balance in your spending and saving habits so that both parts of you are fulfilled.

> *There is no joy in living a life where you deprive yourself of every small joy just to serve future you.*

Future you needs to be taken care of, but we can take care of them while also allowing ourselves to enjoy the moment and live in the present.

Investors in training understand that when it comes to their money habits, it's all about preservation over deprivation.

So how do you do it? Once you have an idea of how much you make and what you spend on a weekly and monthly basis, it's time to examine if this aligns with your value-based spending. Note down how much you spend on your needs, as well as your wants, in alignment with your goals.

If at this point you realise your values and spending aren't in alignment, it's time to sit down and allocate where you want to spend your money so things do start to align. Some people like to use images of things like buckets or hats. Some people like percentages. I just like to use numbers. It does the job. See table 3.1. Take out a pen and jot down roughly how much you make a month and how you'd like to split that across your wants and needs. It'll take you four minutes at most, I promise.

Table 3.1: income allocation

Income (monthly)	$

Home and utilities	
groceries	$
mortgage	$
rates	$
home maintenance	$
internet/phone	$
electricity	$
water	$

Insurance & finance	
savings	$
investments	$
car insurance	$
home & contents	$
life insurance	$
health insurance	$
loan/credit card repayments	$

| pet insurance | $ |
| income protection | $ |

Personal & entertainment	
eating out	$
clothing & shoes	$
grooming (hair, beauty, skincare)	$
gym/sports	$
app subscriptions (e.g. Headspace)	$
music/TV subscriptions	$
holidays	$
gifts/donations	$

Transport	
public transportation fare/taxi costs	$
petrol	$
parking	$
repairs/maintenance	$
car insurance/registration	$
other	$

Children and/or dependents	
babysitting/childcare	$
schooling & activities	$
pet care & vet bills	$
child support payments	$
parental retirement aid/health (e.g. giving your parents money every month to help with their living expenses)	$

Health	
doctor appointments	$
vitamins	$
medication	$
sanitary products	$
other	$

I don't quite believe in asking people to put 30 per cent into one category or 20 per cent in another. Value-based spending means you get to decide what you do with the money you get in your account every week. You may decide to put 50 per cent into your living costs because you prefer to live in a more expensive city to be close to family—that doesn't mean you should be made to feel guilty for not keeping living expenses 'under 30 per cent'. It's all about aligning what's on this paper with what you value in your life.

Once you get a clear picture on that you'll know exactly what you have left to allocate to investing. Someone may say 'This leaves me with $50 left over at the end of the week, but I value holidays so I'm okay with putting $40 of that money into a savings account towards my travel fund, and putting $10 to investing.' That is fine.

You are allowed to decide that travelling means more to you than investing. We are not all the same people, and we have different life experiences and desires. It's just important to note that we can't have it all at the same time; if we want to grow our wealth faster, it's about deciding what our values are and shifting our spending and saving habits to reflect that. One person is going to feel more fulfilled by being wealthy in experiences over money. It's too personal to generalise and shame each other on our money habits.

> *By having a clearer idea of where your money is going, you get to control it rather than having it control you.*

Your spending habits are not an easy thing to face, but you're better off in the long term to have laid down this brick. Well done.

Brick #2: Tackle high-interest debt

Trying to invest while having high-interest debt is like trying to fill a bucket with a hole in it. No matter how much water you put in, whether it be from a glass or water directly from a hose, you will never be able to fill the bucket until you block the hole that's draining your wealth...I mean water. See figure 3.2.

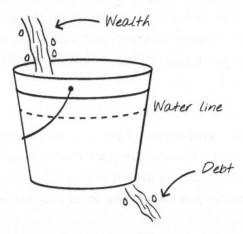

Figure 3.2: high-interest debt drains your bucket

High-interest debt is the hole in your bucket. Let me explain with numbers. If you invest and get a nice 10 per cent return every year but you have a car loan or high-interest credit card debt of the same amount that is taking 15 per cent per annum, you're not making money—in fact you're still losing 5 per cent. In simple terms, if you have $100 a month to either invest or pay off high-interest debt, you're going one step ahead but two steps back by investing it. Getting rid of high-interest debt is an important part of your financial wellness journey and another strong brick in your foundation.

Now, you may be wondering what kinds of debt you should be getting rid of before you invest, and what debt doesn't matter too much.

In countries such as New Zealand, student loans are usually 0 per cent interest, so it does not make sense to pay this off before you begin investing. In fact, when debt has a 0 per cent interest it almost makes sense to pay it off as slowly as possible, as $50 000 today will be worth less in five to 10 years' time due to inflation.

In some countries or with private universities, student loan debt can range from 3 to 14 per cent, and the loans themselves can be as high as six figures. Interest on credit card debt is on average around 14.5 per cent, and mortgages average around 3 to 6 per cent. So which ones do you pay off?

There is no magic number that determines what 'high interest' is, but I like to say that anything over 7 per cent should be paid off sooner rather than later. Why? Because the stock market usually returns 7 to 9 per cent annually, so having debt at or over 7 per cent begins to eat away at your gains. It's just like pouring water into that bucket with the hole at the bottom.

If you have debt, let's list them out:

1. Student loan debt $_____ at ____ per cent

2. Credit card debt $_____ at ____ per cent
    (Look, if you need multiple lines for this one, I am not judging.)

3. Personal loan debt (e.g. car) $_____ at ____ per cent

4. Mortgage debt $_____ at ____ per cent.

If any of these interest rates are higher than 7 per cent, it's worth your time focusing your attention on paying them off as soon as possible—in most circumstances, you'll feel better about investing once you have all the high-interest debt paid off. If the interest rate is under 7 per cent it doesn't mean you cannot invest until the debt is paid off—if that were the case, no one with a mortgage would ever enter the stock market.

To get rid of your high-interest debt, you might be able to start by consolidating or refinancing your debt. This means merging several debts into one and ideally getting a better interest rate to attack them faster. You can achieve this by contacting your bank or credit union or speaking with a financial adviser.

Snowballs and avalanches

If you're more of a DIY person, one way to tackle debt is the snowball method. List all your debt from the smallest amount owing to the largest, then tackle the smallest debts first, working your way up to the largest one. For example, if Ha-eun had $2000 credit card debt on one card, $5000 on another and a $13000 car loan, she'd pay them off in this exact order. This helps to build momentum and is often a good place to start for those who may feel overwhelmed.

Why you'd want to use the snowball method:

- It gives you motivation over every 'small win'.

- Your first debt is paid off sooner.

Another way is the avalanche method, where you tackle the debt with the highest interest rate and then work your way down. In this case Ha-eun would first pay down the loan with the highest interest rate, then the one with the second highest interest rate, and so on. This is a great method for when interest rates are higher, which can grow the debt out of control much faster.

Why you'd use the debt avalanche method:

- If interest rates are high, it stops the debt from growing quickly.

Invest or pay off that mortgage?

A common question I get is how to deal with having a mortgage and wanting to invest. Are you meant to pay off your mortgage first and then invest, or should you do both simultaneously? The short answer is either works.

The long answer is that it depends on the interest rate of the mortgage, how many years are left on the loan, and your personal preferences. Let's imagine you had a $500 000 mortgage with a 5 per cent interest rate for 30 years.

If you had a spare $1000 a month, you could top up your mortgage monthly, which would save you 12 years and eight months off your mortgage and save $212 381 in interest payments. That's a significant chunk of money and time.

Now if you invested $1000 a month for 18 years instead of putting it into your mortgage, with a conservative annual return of 6 per cent, you'd have $380 959 in your investing portfolio, which makes investing a better option than paying off the mortgage. But you'd still have 12 extra years to pay off your mortgage, and as rates change this could eat into your gains.

As a result, one could work just as well as the other depending on your personal circumstances. It's important to note that if you went the investment route, you'd also be taking on the risk of assuming the stock market would perform well over the 18 years, which, while likely, is not guaranteed.

In some countries, interest rates for your mortgage get updated on a regular basis while others can offer the same flat rate for 30 years (US, I'm looking at you). When your interest rates can change, so can your goals. You may decide to not focus on paying off your mortgage fast one year, but change your mind when you refix your new rate.

Some people (like my parents) don't like having debt over their heads and want to get rid of their mortgage as soon as possible. Some people (like me) are okay with a mortgage and instead pay the minimum, putting the rest into the stock market. Both these systems work for the people involved.

There are some situations where, regardless of money, you might prefer to pay off your mortgage first, e.g. if you're closer to retirement and don't want to have those repayments affecting your cash flow. Or wanting to free up your monthly income. At the end of the day, it's about finding what works for you.

Brick #3: Automate your money

I love automation. I love technology. It's arguably one of the best things to have happened to someone lazy like me. One of my older colleagues used to call us the button generation—where everything can happen at the click of a button, from food being delivered to our homes to ordering a taxi. I'll take it.

Our money can be automated too, and it's great. It takes away the stress of having one extra thing to do in your life, especially on days when you feel overwhelmed and have so much on your plate already. Sonya, my best friend and podcast co-host, likes to keep money and investing as simple as possible—after all, if it's already a bit of a difficult concept to learn about, we don't want to make it even harder to do.

Once you decide that you want to invest and you have a good understanding of your cash flow, it's time to open an extra online bank account. You want to set up an automation so that every time you get paid, $X goes into this account. This is your investing account: it's where your investing money sits until you put it into your brokerage account.

For example, say you get paid $900 every week. After accounting for all your needs and wants and your savings, you have $50 left.

You'll have $50 automatically transferred every week into your investing account, and then have the money from there transferred every fortnight or month into your brokerage account to invest.

'Why not invest weekly?' you might ask. Good question.

Many brokers have fees associated, and while we get into fees in a lot more depth in chapter 5, for now let's say that if you're investing with a small amount, like $50 a week, you're better off saving that and investing $100 a fortnight or $200 a month to mitigate the fees. As you can tell, this rule doesn't apply as much if you're investing with a lot more money.

So rather than getting paid, spending what we want and then saving or investing what's left over, we flip the order, putting aside a part of our pay cheque for our future self every time we get paid. It's the definition of paying yourself first. Sonya calls it a form of self-respect and I fully agree. Future you will thank you for it.

Brick #4: Make a rainy day fund

Before we begin investing it's important to have a three-month emergency fund kept in a high-yield savings account. This should cover three months of your living expenses; some people like to be able to cover up to six months of expenses, and I've even met people who keep up to 12 months of living expenses. How many months you have saved up will depend on your risk tolerance and what kind of work you do. For example, freelancers may save up more due to the nature of their job, while a doctor or nurse may not be too concerned about job shortages. It's important to have a savings account for emergencies only.

You can decide what emergencies mean for you (in addition to the obvious, such as sickness or loss of employment). For me it's things like:

- dental work

- private healthcare costs

- car breakdowns

- insurance excess on something stolen.

For me it doesn't include things like:

- fines or parking tickets

- unexpected travel

- upgrading (flights, tickets, etc.) last minute.

Having an emergency fund has been life-changing for me. It's allowed me to have a level of peace in my life that I have not had before. It's a great way to make sure that I am always looked after and always have access to money. If I need to leave a situation that does not serve me, I don't have to rely on someone else to help me out.

I recommend opening up another bank account to keep this emergency fund in, preferably a high-yield savings account that you have easy access to. Some people ask if they should invest this money; the answer is no.

Investors in training understand this isn't money you're trying to make money off; it's money that you're keeping aside but can access instantly. When you invest this kind of money in the stock market, you need to wait for it to liquidate before you can use it, and in the short term this may fluctuate, thus not giving you the full amount of money you need. It's tempting to put your emergency fund into the stock market, but that's greed taking over rationality.

Another benefit of having an emergency fund is so you don't draw down your stocks every time there is an emergency. An investing portfolio shouldn't be treated like another bank account you can pull money from every time you want to make a purchase. By pulling out your money, not only do you trigger fees, but also taxes and the opportunity cost of compound interest.

You don't want to have to sell your stocks every time there is an emergency. By having an account dedicated to emergencies, you're taking care of yourself financially. Save yourself up an emergency fund before you begin investing.

Brick #5: Sort out your retirement account

You may be in the US or UK, in India or New Zealand—wherever in the world you're reading this from, it is almost guaranteed that your employer has a government-issued retirement scheme where your employer matches your contributions (or at least some part of your contributions).

In simple terms, if you sacrifice 3 per cent of your salary to your retirement account, your employer puts the same amount again into that account. That is a 100 per cent return on your money. It is unlikely the stock market or cryptocurrency could ever guarantee a 100 per cent return on investment (ROI).

You may be wondering what the point of this is. The government in your country understands the importance of you having a nest egg for retirement. They don't want you to be without money when you reach 65, so they will ask employers to match your contributions as a way of encouraging you to save.

People often ask how much of their income they should contribute, as most countries offer a range from 3 per cent to even 8 per cent or more. The answer is simple: contribute the minimum amount for maximum employer contribution. If your employer only gives up to 6 per cent, you only match 6 per cent. Otherwise, anything extra you add gets locked into the retirement fund.

The next step is finding out what retirement fund you've been set up with. For most of us this is usually set at a basic balanced fund. Some governments will go out of their way to choose this for you, keeping you in the most conservative fund just in case. However, a balanced or conservative fund isn't always the best fund for you.

If this is a retirement account, usually you don't need this money any time soon, so you may want to choose a growth account, or if you'd prefer less risk, then a balanced account might be a better option. The third option is for those who aren't comfortable with much risk and therefore are okay with less reward. This is when a conservative account comes in.

You may question why you should invest into these accounts when you can just invest that money in the stock market, right? It's that 100 per cent ROI that is important. Also, this money is usually inaccessible until you're 65, or at least until you have a life-altering situation where you need money to get you through an illness. In some countries you can also pull this money out to buy your first home. The benefit of having this fund is that it acts as a literal barrier between us and our money. Sometimes it's a good thing to not have access to it and to let it compound over time until we need it.

Research which retirement option to go with, as there are so many out there. In some countries like New Zealand where it's not compulsory (unlike Australia), you may find that you're not investing into one at all, or that the one you're in isn't aligned with the amount of risk you're comfortable with.

★★★

Congratulations! You now have your first 5 bricks laid out. These are going to be the foundation of your financial future. When it comes to investing in the stock market, investors in training know the importance of having these foundations rock solid before they begin. It's tempting to invest before ticking these off, but I highly recommend you take one evening this week to tick these off—you can get it done in two uninterrupted hours. Investing is a marathon, and if it's an activity you're going to do for the rest of your life, it pays to set it up right before you begin.

Actionable steps

1. Track your spending for a week.

2. Find out what debt you have and fill in the blanks on pages 52-3.

3. Work out how much you can put away every week/month to invest, then make a separate online bank account and automate your money into there.

4. Make a separate online account for your emergency fund.

5. Research your country's top 5 retirement accounts and see what options are available for you.

6. Find out what retirement scheme you have and what 'fund type' you have—does it match your goals?

7. Contribute to your retirement scheme the maximum amount your employer will match.

Investor profile

NAME: Chrissy

AGE: 29

JOB: Public administration

1. What does your investment portfolio look like?

The majority of my portfolio is in my US retirement fund. In my brokerage, my portfolio is currently 50 per cent VTI, 40 per cent AAPL (Apple), and the remainder is split between MSFT (Microsoft), FB (Facebook/Meta), AAL (American Airlines Group Inc) and DIS (Walt Disney Co). I will continue to invest mostly into VTI, but will be adding additional individual stocks in 2022.

2. When did you begin investing and what was your first investment?

Technically 2014/2015 when I signed up for a 403b (part of the US retirement scheme). However, I didn't begin investing seriously until 2018.

3. What stopped you from investing; were there any barriers you had to overcome?

Fear and financial anxiety initially stopped me from investing outside of my employer-sponsored accounts. I was afraid of losing money in the market and watching my account balances fluctuate. Dealing with financial anxiety and analysis paralysis has been the most difficult, but most impactful, part of my investing journey.

4. Any tips for new investors?

The two best pieces of investing advice I've heard are: 1) Never pass up on your employer match, and 2) The sooner you start, the better (because time in the market is so important!). Don't wait until you feel 100 per cent ready. This was incredible advice for me, as someone who often suffers from analysis paralysis.

4

Stock market 101

I once knew an engineer. If you've had the privilege of knowing what engineers are like, you'll know they tend to be very curious. They always want to break things up and piece them back together. The engineer I knew couldn't work out one thing, however: they never could wrap their head around what on earth DNA is. No matter how many times I tried to explain it, they couldn't grasp the fact that DNA is made of wee little building blocks called proteins. These proteins get strung together on a ladder, and the sequence of the rungs of the ladder write your genetic code. Bigger proteins then read your code like a recipe and make you who you are.

DNA to the engineer is what the stock market is to a lot of people. No matter how many times it gets explained, it just doesn't make sense. How does it work? Where does the money go? No matter how many times we try to research it, it can be so hard to grasp. What does it mean, where do the men in suits who shout on the phones come into it? What are all the numbers on the screen and what are those red and green arrows for?

Well, it's time to crack the code about what the stock market is, and what better way to do it than with a classic lemonade stand analogy?

Sim's Lemonade

Imagine I own a lemonade stand. And since I'm a savvy business owner, let's imagine that the stand does extremely well. From the get-go my stand grows immensely: people from far and wide come to buy my lemonade. Business is booming.

But there is only one of me; I only have one stand, and in order to grow, I need to expand to newer markets. One day I decide to open another stand in the next neighbourhood. However, to do so I need another stand, I need more cups, more lemons, and I need to hire someone to manage that stand full time and I need someone to bookkeep. All these things cost money.

Money I don't have. Sure, I could use my profits to do this, but I have a life to live, so that's out of the question.

The next option is getting a loan from a bank, but a loan means paying it back, with interest on top of it. Compound interest is fun when you get the compounding benefits, but it's not so fun when it's a loan you have to pay back.

So what does a business owner like myself do to raise some extra cash? I could sell some shares (or stocks, the two terms mean the same thing) in my company. This means breaking my company into pieces, or shares—it can be any number, 1000 or a million—and then selling these shares to investors.

This process is called an IPO, or initial public offering. It's basically when companies get to shout from the rooftop that they're going from a private company to a public one. Have you ever seen a CEO ringing a bell at the New York Stock Exchange with balloons behind them? This is the moment they officially 'go public'. This is why you can buy shares of some companies, such as Coca-Cola, but not of your locally owned café or fish and chips shop. Coca-Cola is public, but the local fish and chips shop is still a private company.

The benefit of becoming a public company is that I make money from selling shares to investors, and I don't need to pay it back—it's a sweet deal.

When Twitter was expanding, it decided to have an IPO in September 2013. They worked with Goldman Sachs to get it done. (Fun fact, if you ever wondered what on earth investment bankers do, part of their job is to hold the hand of a company through the IPO process, helping them choose what share price to set the IPO at, etc.)

Twitter had not yet turned a profit by the time it was about to launch its IPO, but it ended up being the most anticipated IPO of the year. It was a huge success, raising the company $2.1 billion. It made co-founders Jack Dorsey and Biz Stone instant billionaires. (Another fun fact: Jack Dorsey left Twitter in 2022 to pursue his passion for cryptocurrency.)

The company used a lot of the cash to reinvest in the company, expanding their hardware, acquiring other companies, and majorly re-designing their user interface and their widely successful 'instant timeline'. By investing back into their brand with their IPO money, Twitter was able to establish itself as the technology giant that it is today. And they didn't have a loan to pay back. No wonder companies are so eager to go public!

So back to my lemonade stand. We're no Twitter but we want to grow, and preferably without taking a loan from a bank. Having debt is a bad idea for my business, so instead I announce to the world I am going public, get into the press to create some hype around the IPO and prepare as the launch date approaches.

The day we go public, I break my company into 1000 pieces. I keep 600 pieces myself so that I keep majority ownership and sell each remaining piece, or share, for $10. I have 400 of these to sell, $4000 worth.

At the IPO there are investors like yourself who look at my $10 a share offer. They think my company has potential to grow in the future and can see the value of these shares increasing in the future, so they buy a share.

The money from these initial investors gives me $4000 to open up many lemonade stands. It's important to note that from here onwards, any buying or selling of my lemonade stand shares doesn't come to my company anymore; I've made my money. If person A now buys one of these shares off person B, the one who profits is person B. Any company you invest in doesn't directly receive that money; rather, it goes to the person you're buying the share from.

Let's say one of the original investors in the lemonade stand is called Sally. Sally has one share of my lemonade stand. It's not something she physically owns but rather can be thought of like an online certificate. She bought the share from my IPO for $10 because she believes the value of the share will be up to $20 in five years.

Another investor called Rita comes into the picture. She thinks that the value of the lemonade stand is $20 a share already and offers to buy the share off Sally for $20. Sally is stoked, so she sells her share to Rita and profits $10.

Why would Rita do this? Well, she believes that the share is likely to be worth $30 in five years, so she doesn't mind paying a bit more.

Then another investor called Nancy comes into the scene. Nancy thinks the stock is actually worth $15, lower than what Rita has paid. Nancy offers to buy the lemonade stand stock off Rita for $15. Rita doesn't have to say yes, but the idea that she's holding onto something that she may have overpaid for scares Rita and causes her to panic-sell it to Nancy. Nancy now owns the stock for $15 and Rita has lost $5 on her investment.

This buying and selling of my lemonade stock between investors is what the stock market is. That's it. (We get into more of the finer details, such as why stock prices move, in chapter 7.)

The stock market is just a facilitator that allows people to buy and sell shares amongst each other. It's like eBay, where on one side is someone trying to purchase the product and on the other side is the seller trying to sell the product, only in the stock market the 'product' is shares. It really is that simple. (If you'd like a more technical explanation, the stock market is a group of exchanges where the buying, selling and issuance of stocks—as in, creating stocks—occurs.)

I cannot even begin to explain to you how angry I got when I finally understood what the stock market was.

For so many years it came across as this big scary beast that was too technical for me to understand. And yet now a lecturer is telling me the stock market is just eBay for shares of companies? Are you freaking kidding me? Unfortunately, no jokes were being made. And to add injury to the insult, not everyone gets told the truth as early as I did. It frustrates me how many of us go around completely unaware of how simple the concepts of growing our wealth are, and how largely inaccessible this information has been.

Tulips and the world's first IPO

Long before Twitter went public, the world's first modern IPO occurred in March 1602. The company was the Dutch East India Company (or alternatively VOC, short for its Dutch name, *Vereenigde Oost-Indische Compagni*). It was part of a movement of exploration around the world, and at the time, this company was worth more than some of today's largest companies, like Apple, Google and Facebook, combined. When you account for inflation, this company would be worth around $7 trillion in today's money.

They became very successful for spice trading in the Republic of Indonesia. The Dutch had a monopoly with their government that lasted over 20 years and helped keep them as an attractive option to investors—after all, when you see a government jump in to help a private company stay afloat, investors often assume the company is less likely to fail.

They decided they'd offer shares to the general public through the Amsterdam Stock Exchange to help fund their business, becoming the first publicly listed company to sell shares to retail investors (people like you and me). They raised 6.5 million guilders to then fund their explorations. It was a successful IPO to say the least.

I do want to take a moment to acknowledge that when we speak about history, we cannot erase the problems with explorations such as these. The Dutch East India Company also engaged in the trading of enslaved people and displacing African and Asian people as part of its business model. It was entirely unethical and inhumane, and had lasting effects on the economies and wealth of the countries they targeted.

The Dutch East India Company also played a huge role in the stock market's first economic bubble. A bubble, like the Dotcom Bubble mentioned in chapter 2, is when the price of something keeps getting higher and higher based on speculation, ultimately becoming unsustainable and quickly dropping in price. But the first bubble wasn't actually based around a single stock—it was about flowers. Tulips, to be exact.

I've never come across a bunch of tulips I haven't considered beautiful, but my feelings towards them pale in comparison to those of the Dutch in the sixteenth century. They were so prized that, at the peak of the bubble, some tulip bulbs were being sold for six times the average person's annual salary at the time.

It all began when tulips were imported into Europe from Turkey thanks to the spice trade routes. They were seen as a status symbol because they were so fragile. Originally only a prize for the wealthy, they quickly became popular among the middle class as well. All types of tulips were being traded, with multicoloured ones perceived as being even rarer and more valuable. By 1634 'Tulip Mania', as it was called, had truly swept through the country.

It felt like the price of tulips could only go higher, and many people were making a pretty penny from buying and selling the flowers. The bubble became obvious when people started taking loans to buy tulips, as they were so confident that prices were only going higher and higher. Charles Mackay wrote in his book *Extraordinary Popular Delusions and the Madness of Crowds* that at one point 12 acres of land were offered for a single tulip bulb.

When accounting for inflation, tulips were selling for the equivalent of US$50 000 to as high as US$700 000 in today's market. It was madness. And of course, like all speculative bubbles, it eventually burst.

In three years' time many, unfortunately, found themselves holding stock of tulips that people were no longer interested in. It was a definite moment in the market, demonstrating how humans behave during a bubble, and it still holds as a reminder of how human behaviour can change when lured by the possibility of making a quick return.

When markets begin to rise unexpectedly in current times, you may notice people will start to reference Tulip Mania as a warning of a possible bubble forming again.

Bubbles are usually formed when people stop seeing the intrinsic value of a company or stock and instead get overwhelmed by the fear of missing out. It's a common phenomenon that will continue to occur in the market, but the investor in training is aware that when greed seeps in, the fundamentals of investing are often pushed to the side.

While the Amsterdam Stock Exchange was growing strong in the 1600s (and it's still the oldest surviving stock exchange in the world), many others were beginning to form in the busiest cities around the world.

Stock exchanges = stock market? Not quite

A stock exchange is a location where stocks or shares are exchanged, i.e. bought and sold. There are many stock exchanges around the world, many in the most prominent cities of large countries. In fact, there are 60 exchanges worldwide. Out of these, 16 of them are extremely large, with the value of the companies listed on each of these large exchanges being over $1 trillion. These larger exchanges account for 87 per cent of the value of the global stock market and are all located in Asia, North America or Europe. That's probably a lot of words, so let me break it down.

Think of a stock exchange like a list. Most countries have just one list. It lists all the companies that you can buy stocks in. This lets you see how much the price of that company stock is and how much the price has changed since yesterday.

So how is the stock exchange or list different to the stock market? Well, the stock market can be made up of a number of exchanges. For example, the US stock market is made up of 13 US exchanges, such as their famous New York Stock Exchange or the NASDAQ exchange (see figure 4.1), whereas the global stock market is made up of all 60 exchanges in the world.

Back in the day, before stock exchanges existed, investors used to gather in person to discuss and exchange investments. Sometimes it would be at a coffee shop in London, or at a park in the US.

New York City was booming in the eighteenth century, and investors and brokers would often meet under a buttonwood tree to do deals. The tree was the most perfect spot, situated close to the financial district and banks. What was the name of the street the tree was located at? Wall Street.

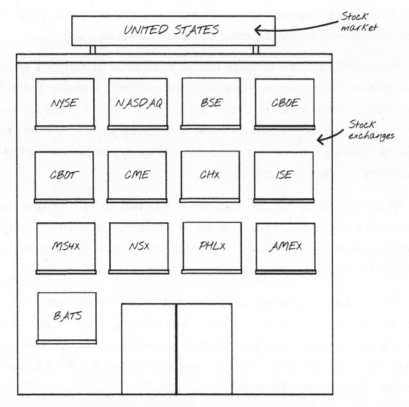

Figure 4.1: the US stock market

Wall Street became home to the New York Stock Exchange (NYSE) in 1792, with 24 founding stockbrokers, where they fittingly named their contract the Buttonwood Agreement.

Initially, ownership of the exchange was extremely exclusive, and you could only obtain a membership by purchasing a seat from an existing member. The first company to be listed was the Bank of New York. The NYSE has now become one of the world's most famous stock exchanges, and to this date is still the biggest powerhouse in the stock market.

If you go to the NYSE today you'll see that, even though modern technology allows the average person to invest online, there are still traders that run around on the trading floor. We don't technically need human traders to execute deals or make trades anymore thanks to technology, however, keeping the trading floor open continues as a sort of tradition. It also provides news sources great visual content of panicked and stressed-out traders for when the stock market drops slightly.

Remember that an exchange can be thought of as simply a list of companies. Companies are limited to the exchange that lists them. If you want to invest in British Petroleum you'd invest through the London Stock Exchange. If you want to invest in Samsung you'd go through the Korea Exchange. Whichever company you want, you have to find the exchange it comes from and go there.

Thankfully, gone are the days when you had to call brokers that worked on these exchanges in order to invest. (As a millennial who's petrified of phone calls, I hate to admit this was one of the barriers that stopped me from investing for a long time.)

Instead there are things called online brokers. We get into brokers in 'Putting it all together', but the main takeaway here is that stock exchanges hold the companies you're interested in, the stock market is made up of the exchanges and you invest in the stock market through brokers. Simple—see figure 4.2.

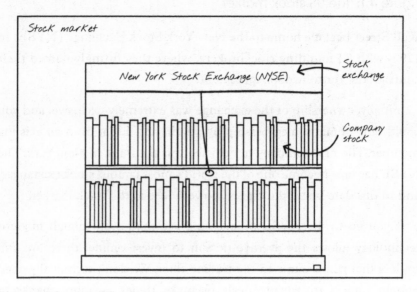

Figure 4.2: simplified stock market

The stock market, though it appears complex and intricate, is really quite simple. The industry has done an amazing job at complicating it and using jargon to push people out. It reminds me a lot of the type of girl in high school who wouldn't tell you where she got her dress from. Except now you can take a photo of the dress and use an app to scan online clothing shops (or, in our case, read a book about investing and have it broken down for us). The beauty of this modern world is that the walls of secrecy built around industries are beginning to collapse, opening them up to everyday people who want to learn about how to build generational wealth. Now that these walls are falling, it's time to step in.

Actionable steps

If you can explain a complex concept simply, it means you've grasped it well. In that spirit:

1. Try explaining to a friend what the stock market is.

2. Try explaining to a friend what an IPO is.

Investor profile

NAME: Sarah

AGE: 23

JOB: Host of podcast *OneUp Project*

1. What does your investment portfolio look like?

My portfolio is 95 per cent in funds spread across the US, NZ and AUS top 500/100/50 and funds such as the Vanguard S&P 500. The other 5 per cent is Tesla and a teeny tiny Bitcoin holding.

2. When did you begin investing?

March 2020 (classic COVID timing).

3. What stopped you from investing; were there any barriers you had to overcome?

Absolutely! I thought it was for people who had a lot of money and were really well educated. I felt too poor and stupid to get involved earlier, which is a truly sad thing to admit.

4. Any tips for new investors?

The best time to invest was yesterday, the second best time is now. Getting started is always the hardest but most crucial part!

5

What's your type (of investment)?

Let's get into what it's like using the stock market to grow wealth.

A good place to start is to understand what investing is. In its simplest form, investing is the process of putting your money into something with an expectation that it will make a return. The word 'expectation' is important; it's not guaranteed that you'll make a return on your money, even though that's the only point of investing. You could put that money into real estate, a stock or even into a Birkin bag collection; all of these are forms of investing, because money is being allocated with the goal of not only getting your money back but making a return as well.

That's it.

Investing is just the idea that you throw some money into something, and you hope more money comes out.

No men in suits in sight.

There are many different ways to invest your money, but I'm going to break down the most popular ones you'll come across:

- stocks/shares

- bonds

- mutual funds

- index funds

- ETFs

- REITs (real estate investment trusts)

- hedge funds

- commodities and alternative investments.

Stocks/shares

Firstly, 'shares' and 'stocks' are interchangeable terms. In North America they're often referred to as stocks, while 'down under' we go by shares.

A share is simply a small piece of a company; when a company sells a portion of its ownership, it does so by issuing stocks/shares. When someone says 'I'm investing in Apple' it means the same thing as 'I'm buying Apple shares'. It also means 'I'm a shareholder of Apple'.

Having a small piece of a company technically makes you a shareholder of a company, meaning you own that small portion of the company. So if you bought a share of Apple and Twitter today, you'd own part (albeit a tiny part) of these companies. Better update your LinkedIn profile.

By being a shareholder of any company, you get to reap the rewards of that business's success: if it makes a profit you may get paid dividends, and if the company does well, the stock price usually goes up over time. But this also means you get to deal with the downfalls of a company; when the company lands in hot water, its price can sometimes falter too.

For example, when you buy $1000 worth of Boeing shares, there is a risk that your $1000 is going to drop if a Boeing plane has a malfunction that reflects poorly on the company.

Shares are known to be a bit volatile compared to the other investing types we'll get into, such as funds or bonds. It's because they are at their core just one investment type. When it comes to the saying 'don't put all your eggs in one basket', it's often referring to the idea that it may not be wise to only hold shares of one company in your entire portfolio. Even five companies aren't enough, but we'll get into that in chapter 9 when we speak about diversifying.

Shareholders also get to have a say in how the company runs, but to a pretty small scale. You can go to shareholder meetings, although these are often virtual, and vote on how the company is run.

The voting includes stock-standard items such as electing the board of directors. Yes, that's right, you can technically vote Larry Page off Google's board. Their 2021 meeting, for example, voted on appointing their accounting firm, Ernst and Young, and whether they should add a human rights and/or civil rights expert to the board. (Interestingly enough, there were more votes against it than for it.) You don't have to go to these meetings, but I highly recommend attending one for the sake of it. And yes, they're over Zoom.

Stocks are broken down into a range of categories, but the six most common are as follows:

- **Growth stocks:** These are usually tech companies that are trying to grow quicker than the rest of the stocks in their sector. These are like potential romantic partners that are a bit wild and spontaneous; you don't know what you're going to get and you may crash and burn. High risk with the potential for high reward.

- **Blue Chip stocks:** These are the partners your parents want you to end up with. They're established, stable and reliable, with a strong reputation (e.g. Disney stock).

- **Sector stocks:** Stocks can be broken down by sector, such as stocks in healthcare (e.g. pharmacy companies), utilities, IT, energy, pharmaceuticals, materials, financials and consumer discretionaries or staples.

- **Large cap stocks:** Market capitalisation is how much a company is worth (e.g. $1 billion or $5 billion). Companies that are worth over $10 billion are large cap. Stocks in large cap companies tend to be more stable, but don't grow as fast (e.g. Alphabet stock).

- **Mid cap stocks:** Companies with a market capitalisation between $2 and $10 billion. They're a mixture of the benefits and drawbacks you'd see in both large cap and small cap stocks. The best of both worlds, as Hannah Montana would say.

- **Small cap stocks:** Companies with a market capitalisation of less than $2 billion. These stocks are the most volatile but can provide high reward for high risk. They're essentially like startups. Most fail but some 'shoot to the moon' and provide great returns.

Stocks can be thought of as the purest form of investing: choosing a company and putting your money on the line to back them.

Bonds

If stocks are the party animals of the world, bonds are the studious, quiet types. They don't bother anyone, they do what they say they'll do, and, sadly, they're often left out of the equation until things start to fall apart.

Bonds are when you get to act like a bank and loan your money to a government or company. With bonds, the company or government are basically asking you to loan them money. They'll pay it back to you with a fixed amount of interest to say thank you for letting them borrow it. In fancy terms bonds are a debt instrument (think of an 'instrument' like a service) representing a loan by you, the investor, to a borrower, such as a government.

Companies and organisations use the money raised through bonds to finance their work. Companies issue corporate bonds and governments issue municipal bonds, but the way they both work is very much the same. The bond rates are affected by interest rates, so when interest rates rise, people tend to buy more bonds. You buy your bond at an agreed interest rate, then you get paid your fixed interest (e.g. 2 per cent) no matter what the climate of the world is, unlike shares where the returns you get fluctuate. After the agreed amount of time, you get your initial money back. This initial money is called your principal.

Bonds are much less risky than stocks. One way I remember this is thinking 'the government can't *not* pay me back if I lend them money—it'll make them look bad!' However, due to the lower risk of them ghosting you, they give you a lower return on your money. You'll notice this trend a lot through this book: if you want to increase your chance of making more gains, you need to factor in more risk. Investors in training know they can't quite have their cake and eat it too.

Mutual funds

Rather than holding your money in individual companies, you can put a bunch of companies together in a basket and invest in a piece of that basket, called a fund. This is where mutual funds come in. Mutual funds (also known as managed funds) are baskets that can be filled with many different combinations of stocks, bonds, cash or cash equivalents, and other investments.

Some mutual funds have these companies chosen by a computer (e.g. an index fund), while other mutual funds are actively managed by a human being. For the purpose of this book, when I say 'mutual funds',

I'm referring to actively managed mutual funds, as that is what most personal finance jargon refers to. But technically mutual funds are just a management style. A mutual fund can be an actively managed fund as well as a passive index fund. Technically it is incorrect to assume all mutual funds are actively managed, but for the purpose of simplicity we'll assume the mutual funds we speak about are in fact actively managed.

Mutual funds pool money from many investors and invest them on their behalf. One mutual fund could be a basket of tech stocks or energy stocks. It could be a basket of high-growth companies or more stable companies. You can buy a 'share' of a mutual fund in the same way that you can buy a share of a company; only instead of buying a piece of a company, you're buying a piece of the basket of stocks. (It's worth noting these funds don't always have to invest in stocks—they can also be made up of bonds or other types of investments.)

How do actively managed mutual funds choose their stocks? Imagine a person is tasked with the job of selecting the best berries on a farm. They examine the berries and clear them of anything that makes them unattractive, thus screening through all the berries and only putting the best ones in the basket. This is what the fund manager is trying to do. It is someone's full-time job to screen hundreds of companies to try and find the ones that are going to beat the average returns you'd get from the stock market.

Because mutual funds involve people who spend time doing a lot of work, and need offices and spaces to work, these funds tend to have higher fees. Fund managers on average take a 1.4 per cent fee of a portfolio. This may not seem like a lot, but the fee is taken regardless of whether the fund makes you a profit. They are also a lot higher than what you'd be paying in a fund that isn't actively managed, which can sit as low as 0.03 per cent.

Let me tell you a little secret. It's human nature to assume that actively managed funds are more likely to do well, since the fund managers do so much work analysing companies and charge high fees. That's how things are meant to work right? The higher the fee, the more work put in, the better the outcome?

Funnily enough, mutual funds have a lot in common with high-end moisturisers: the cheaper ones do just as well, if not better.

Mutual funds can sometimes do better in the short term, but rarely in the long term. In fact, a study done in 2018 by Standard and Poor's (S&P) Research Group found that over a 15-year investment horizon, only 2.3 to 7.57 per cent of actively managed mutual funds beat the passive index funds (which we'll get into next). Actively managed funds are managed by professionals, who are highly qualified and skilled, equipped with the best software in the world to try and beat the market, and only 2.3 to 7.57 per cent actually get it right.

Investors in training know that despite costing more in fees, actively managed mutual funds usually do as well as or worse than index funds that are cheaper and require less time in research—a fund manager spending 50 hours a week to find the best companies to invest in is spending a lot more time than a passively managed index fund.

Index funds

Index funds are like that humble, low-key friend who is actually a secret superhero, volunteering all their time at the hospital and making you care packages when you're sick. Index funds used to be the overlooked part of the investing world. Funnily enough, they were invented by someone who was sick of mutual funds.

John Bogle, the founder of the Vanguard Group, which is now one of the world's most popular investment management companies, decided to create a type of mutual fund that stripped away all the active investing and instead made it as passive as possible. Though, mind you, Vanguard still has some actively managed funds to this day!

In 1976, Bogle decided that computers were the solution and, rather than relying on someone to spend hours trying to decide what companies to invest in, an automatic system could do it better.

Bogle proposed that instead of trying to beat the market, why not try and *be* the market? His index fund, which was essentially a basket made of the top 500 companies in the US, now called the S&P 500, ended up becoming a huge success.

See, an index fund follows an index, which is just a list. You could follow the top 200 companies in Australia, with an index called the ASX 200, or the top 50 companies in New Zealand, called the NZ 50. You could follow the top 100 companies in the UK, called the FTSE 100, or the top 100 companies in India, the NIFTY 100—the options of indexes are limitless. They also don't have to be a list of top companies; you can have funds that follow a list of only female-run companies, or a list of the top ethical companies in the US.

The three most common indexes are the S&P 500, the Dow Jones Industrial Average, which follows the top 30 companies in the US, and NASDAQ, which follows the top 1000 tech companies in the US. These funds are often quoted to represent when the market moves (e.g. 'the Dow is down 3 per cent'). See figure 5.1.

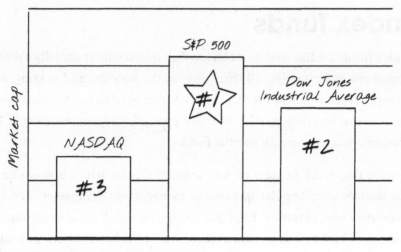

Figure 5.1: the top three indexes

You may have heard of an S&P 500 index fund. Different companies have their own funds based on the index, like Vanguard's S&P 500 fund or Smartshares' S&P 500 fund. They both invest in the same thing. It's like buying a plain black Nike shirt versus an identical plain black Adidas shirt: it's the same black shirt, just different branding. You can buy the fund through a broker (like buying the shirt through Asos or The Iconic) or from its investment company (e.g. buying the shirt directly from Nike or Adidas). In simple terms, these index funds are the world's most common funds and there are many variations of where and how to buy them—but more on that in 'Putting it all together'.

An index fund is a type of mutual fund, but it's passively managed rather than actively managed. If company A surges in value and becomes a top 500 company, the portfolio automatically gets adjusted by investing into company A and kicking out company B, which was #500 on the list but is now #501.

It's simple. Since there's no need to have a person there to adjust the funds and go over which companies should and shouldn't be there, the fees associated with managing index funds are significantly lower. We like lower fees.

Both index funds and mutual funds have a high cost to entry, with mutual funds being the higher of the two. It's not uncommon to see a mutual fund that still asks for a $10000 minimum entry into the fund, though you're more likely to see them asking around $1000 to $5000 to begin with.

And because you're investing in a basket of shares, rather than owning the shares directly, you don't have voting rights. (Look, it was unlikely that your one vote was going to push Larry Page off the Google executive board anyways.)

While index funds are technically a kind of mutual fund, in the general sense, when they are spoken about in the world of investing, most people refer to 'mutual funds' when they speak about actively managed funds and they refer to index funds as passive funds. Investors either love actively managed funds or passive index funds. They either believe actively chosen funds are going to provide them better outcomes in the long term, or that passive funds do better long term. While the evidence shows that the vast majority of actively managed funds do not outperform the index, some do. There's a wide range of reasons why someone may prefer to invest with an actively managed fund, but the most common come down to assuming that the higher cost must equate to better returns, the 'human' element of a fund manager, and the ability to quickly react to the market when things change.

A downside of index funds and mutual funds in general is that their price is valued at the end of the day, and buying/selling of these funds occur after the stock market closes for the day. This means if you wanted to invest at 9 am, you wouldn't be able to. And since index funds often have a minimum investment, you'd need to save up until you could deposit this money (e.g. if you have $100 but the fund is currently valued at $1000, you have to wait and save up $1000 before you can invest in that fund).

In the same way index funds were created to solve a problem, so were ETFs.

ETFs

ETFs or exchange-traded funds, like myself, were introduced in the mid 1990s. They are similar to index funds, and ETFs can often invest in the exact same fund an index would.

In fact, more often than not, you can find an ETF that *tracks* an index fund. ETFs are like shadows to index funds.

For example, a Vanguard S&P 500 index fund also has a Vanguard S&P 500 ETF.

If the index fund goes up 10 per cent, so does the ETF.

If the index fund goes down 9 per cent, so does the ETF.

They invest in the same thing—so why do ETFs exist when index funds do the same job?

There are two important reasons:

1. lower barrier to entry

2. you can buy and sell throughout the day, not just when the market has closed.

Remember that idea of fractional shares, where can you buy a small per cent of one share for as little as $1? That's the same with ETFs. ETFs bypass the minimum $1000 usually needed to buy into index funds. You get to buy a fraction of the basket at a fraction of the cost. This is helpful when you have less money to invest with, and don't want to only be investing every time you save up $1000. With ETFs you can invest in those baskets with $10 or even $1 if you wished to.

The other issue with index funds and mutual funds in general is that they give you one price every day, and you take it or leave it. With ETFs, however, their price varies throughout the day. This also means you can sell it or buy it throughout the day. It's not a huge bother, but it's one of the main differences between index funds and ETFs.

Since ETFs are fan favourites, there are quite a few types of ETFs out there. Let's go over some of the common ones:

- **market ETFs:** they invest in indexes, like the S&P 500

- **bond ETFs:** you can buy a basket of bonds (remember bonds as those loans you give to governments or organisations) as an ETF

- **sector ETFs:** these are ETFs that invest in just one sector, like a basket of just healthcare companies or a basket of just car companies; the most common type is a basket of tech companies

- **foreign market ETFs:** these let you invest in overseas companies outside of your home country

- **actively managed ETFs:** yup, to throw everything you've just learned into the gutter, sometimes ETFs can be actively managed too. They're not always following an index fund. These ETFs are basically like actively managed mutual funds, but you can buy a per cent of them and their price varies throughout the day. Ark Innovative ETFs are currently the most well-known actively managed ETFs on the market. Created by Cathie Wood, their goal is to try and beat the market ETFs by investing in emergent technology, such as stem cell research.

Funds (or baskets) can be used to hold more than just companies; they can also be used for real estate. Enter REITs.

REITs

REITs, or real estate investment trusts, are the funds of the real estate world. Rather than investing in a basket of companies, you now get to invest in a basket of real estate: usually commercial real estate, which is real estate that businesses hire for their companies or stores, rather than homes or apartments where people live.

REITs are a great way for people to get some exposure into the world of real estate without being a landlord. You don't have to manage the real estate, you don't have to deal with contracts or tenants. It doesn't matter if there is a leak in the roof—that is all dealt with.

REITs are also a good option for those who are uncomfortable with the idea of directly being a landlord for private property. By choosing commercial real estate REITs, the younger generations are expressing their moral stance in not owning rental homes. This book is not to judge or make that decision for you, but if you wish to step into real estate, REITs can be a good alternative.

REITs can be bought as mutual funds or as an ETF. Like ETFs, they can also be broken down into sectors. You may prefer to invest in just resorts or hospitals, or just in retail (e.g. a REIT made out of malls).

The reason REITs can be an attractive option is that they provide high-yield dividends, which can be thought of as the equivalent of rent. Rather than buying a commercial property yourself and getting rent from a tenant, you buy a REIT and get a dividend. Some stocks provide dividends too, but REITs do this on a larger scale.

In the last 10 years, the performance of US REITs based on the FTSE NAREIT Equity REIT Index was 9.5 per cent. That's a mouthful, but what it means is that the return was less than or equal to what the broad stock market brought over that 10-year period, so it shouldn't replace your entire portfolio.

It's worth noting that when it comes to physical real estate, 'real' real estate investing often beats out a 9.5 per cent gain, if you leverage. Leverage is the fancy word to say you're using the bank's money to grow your money. For example, say you owned a $500 000 home and you put down a $50 000 deposit. If the house went up 10 per cent the next year, you made a 10 per cent return on the total value of the house, not a 10 per cent return on your $50 000 deposit. This would leave you with a $50 000 return on the original $50 000 you put down. Whereas if you had invested $50 000 in the share market and made a 10 per cent gain, that is only on the $50 000 invested. This would leave you with a $5000 return on your original $50 000 you put down. Leverage can be powerful.

So if you're looking to make big money through real estate, REITs aren't the way to do it. But if you're looking to diversify your stock market portfolio with real estate, REITs fit in quite nicely.

Another benefit of REITs is that, unlike buying or selling physical real estate yourself, which is a process that can take a few months or even a year, REITs are easy to buy and sell. You can have your money in real estate while having a lot more liquidity. (I like to think of liquidity like literal liquid; the more liquidity an investment type has, the easier it is to 'swish around' from one account to another.)

One thing to note about REITs is that they're more sensitive to interest rates and can drop quickly when rates rise. In some countries such as the US, their dividends are also taxed at a higher rate than the dividends of stocks.

Hedge funds

Most people, whether they have invested or not, have heard of the mysterious, exclusive hedge fund.

Hedge funds used to really confuse me. The first time I heard of them I thought they were related to hedges or gated communities. Then I felt like maybe they were so hard to get into because they were protected by 'hedges'. You couldn't have paid me to guess what a hedge fund did.

Eventually I learned that, in essence, hedge funds are just mutual funds—but on steroids. They are run by investment fund managers who are allowed to make riskier investments on behalf of their investors in the hope that they outperform the market average. This means they get to invest in ways that normal investors don't always have access to, unless we have a net worth of more than $1 million.

A hedge fund is still a basket, but rather than a basket just filled with some companies that the fund managers think will do better, it's filled with shinier, newer, more interesting and riskier products that they hope will do better, such as investing in real estate, derivatives or even currencies, among other 'riskier' asset types. If our S&P 500 index fund was a straw basket, a hedge fund is a gold-plated Hermès Birkin bag.

As a result, hedge funds are notoriously expensive to invest in. They also take a whoppingly high cut of profits—20 per cent. It makes the 1 to 2 per cent cut from mutual fund managers look like pennies. In fact, the top 15 hedge fund managers together earned an estimated $23.2 billion in 2020 during the COVID pandemic, according to Bloomberg News. The head of Tiger Global Management alone made $3 billion. Not bad for a pandemic year.

Whether it's a straw basket or a Birkin bag, it actually doesn't matter how much the bag costs (or how much the fees are)—what truly matters is what's inside.

A hedge fund's main purpose is to maximise returns and remove as much risk as possible.

They're called hedge funds, not because of anything related to plants, but rather due to a technique called 'hedging'. You may have heard people say they're 'hedging their bets', meaning they're trying to minimise their risk. Hedging is an investment technique to offset the risk of other investments. For example, if you invest in Apple in the hope that it goes up, you can also hedge your bet so that if it goes down in price, you still make money regardless.

Hedge funds basically try to make money regardless of whether the market goes up or down. It's kind of clever.

So are they worth the hype and all those fees?

In 2008, Warren Buffett, one of the most successful stock market investors in the world, made a 10-year bet to see if hedge funds could beat someone investing in the S&P 500. Warren chose Vanguard's S&P 500 Admiral fund (an index fund that goes by the ticker VFIAX). (A ticker is a symbol made up of two to five letters given to every stock or fund, a bit like a car numberplate, e.g. GOOG for Google.)

Buffett believed that including fees, costs and expenses, passive investing into the S&P 500 was a better strategy than active investing, given their notoriously high fees and the lack of data that supports active investing. Buffett found a hedge fund, Protégé Partners, to take on the bet. The loser would have to donate $1 million to charity. So who would win: the passive index fund or the exclusive and prestigious hedge fund?

In May of 2017, several months before the competition ended, the hedge fund owner wrote an open letter: 'the game is over, I lost'.

It was a huge shock to the investment industry that a passive fund with a fee of 0.04 per cent could outperform a hedge fund that would be charging 2 per cent in fees and 20 per cent of profits. Billions are poured into the hedge fund industry, and yet a passive investor with access to an S&P 500 index fund or ETF could outperform hedge funds? Phenomenal.

It again highlighted the misconception that to make money in the stock market you need a lot of money to start with, or that you need to do a lot of work to invest. It just isn't true, and the sooner investors in training realise that they do not need a net worth of $1 million to begin investing, the better.

Now that we have the most popular investment types down, are there any other investments to consider?

Commodities and alternative investments

To put it simply, commodities are types of investments that help provide more diversification and they help to hedge against inflation. We don't like inflation in the stock market as it can cause stock prices to pull down. It sounds a bit counterintuitive as inflation is known to raise prices of goods and services—but for a company, this means more costly materials and thus lower profits, hence lower share prices.

Commodities are stocks in physical things: metals like gold and silver, agricultural products like wheat and livestock, and energy like crude oil and natural gas. You can buy commodities directly, and the most common way to do so is through stocks or funds (e.g. an energy ETF).

Alternative investments

While traditional investing methods include stocks, bonds and cash, alternative methods include non-traditional approaches to investing. (Technically, hedge funds are alternative investments but I felt like they deserved a section of their own.)

Items such as art, cars, handbags, cryptocurrency and NFTs (the latter two are covered more in chapter 11) are also alternative investments.

That's right. Even luxury bags can be alternative investments. Hermès Birkin bags are so rare they can outperform the market. A crocodile skin Birkin, which can cost anywhere between $60 000 and $200 000, can see an annual return of 14.2 per cent. According to BagHunter, Birkin bags have outperformed the S&P 500 for the last 35 years. The most expensive purchase was a white gold and diamond Birkin selling for $372 000 in 2016. (Now it makes sense why Kris Jenner's wardrobe features a neon sign saying 'Need Money for Birkin'.)

For an investor in training, alternative investments are something we shouldn't be giving too much attention to at the start, especially as the barrier to entry is high. Most of us don't start out with $10 000 to put into a luxury bag or a Picasso piece.

★★★

In the world of investing, there are many types of investments that investors in training have access to—from index funds to ETFs, REITs to commodities. Once broken down in easy-to-understand language, the structure of these investments is digestible even for the most novice investor.

Actionable steps

1. See if you can recall the difference between an index fund and an ETF.

2. Note down two investment types that interest you from what we've covered.

3. Note down the definition of the three most common indexes:

   - the S&P 500

   - the Dow

   - NASDAQ.

Investor profile

NAME: Lindsay (pseudonym)

AGE: 27

JOB: Forestry professional

SALARY: NZ$79 000

1. What does your investment portfolio look like?

Total invested over five years is $46 623. It's 4 per cent Air NZ, 5 per cent ANZ, 22 per cent DIV, 36 per cent FNZ, 2 per cent GNE, 2 per cent OZY, 2 per cent USF, 2 per cent WBC, 16 per cent Forest Block, 9 per cent my company.

2. How much and how often do you invest?

$1000 per month since I was 22 or 23 and started living with my partner.

3. Why do you invest?

To help prepare for my future and retirement, provide for children. Financial stability is the big one.

4. Any tips for new investors?

Have an emergency fund.

6

Hello, stock market millionaire

Everyone would like to be a millionaire, but what does that really mean? When you look deeper into it, you realise everyone wants the freedom of a millionaire. Not everyone wants a big house or a private jet; not everyone needs 10 bathrooms in their homes or fancy clothes. When people say they want to be millionaires, what they really mean is they want to have the freedom to do what they want, and that often involves time.

So how do you get more time? To have more freedom of time you need more money, but to get more money you need more time. This is where investing comes in.

How the stock market can make you money

Let's forget about the millions for a moment and get started with a basic question: how do you make money through the stock market?

There are two ways to make money in the stock market—capital gains and dividends.

Capital gains

Capital gains are simple to understand. If you bought a home for $500000 and it sold for $600000, you made a capital gain of $100000.

It's the same story with the stock market: if you buy an Apple share for $150 and sold it at $160, you've made $10 in capital gains.

You may be thinking: '$10 isn't really helping me on my way to retiring a millionaire though, is it?'

And you'd be correct. Usually it takes a few years, with that beautiful thing called compound interest, before you start to see some really big capital gains in your investing portfolio. For example, if you invested $1000 in Apple at its IPO in 1982 and cashed in now, you'd have a 203000 per cent return on your money. Or even more recently, if you had spent $1000 in 2001 on Apple stocks, you would have turned that into $500000 in 20 years.

Until you sell those stocks, though, the capital gains aren't money in your pocket. This is called unrealised gains. It's basically like having a $500000 home that's worth $600000 now. You don't see that $100000 in cash in your account until you sell it. Investors often wonder about the best time to sell shares. Investors in training understand that, as a long-term investor, you don't sell shares as soon as they bring up capital gains; you hold on to them until you have reached your investing goal. For most of us, that goal is saving up for an earlier retirement, buying a home or putting money away for our children/family. It's not about making a quick buck in the market; it's about playing the long game.

Capital gains are what younger investors usually go for due to having more time on their side, making capital gains more likely. But other investors who want cash flow, aka a lump sum hitting their bank account four times a year, invest for dividends.

Dividends

Dividends are the other way you make money in the stock market, and they're a true form of passive income. It's basically how a company says thank you for holding their stocks in your portfolio; they pay you a small per cent of their profits, usually every quarter. The company's board of directors decides how much dividend to give, and they try and keep it consistent every time. And you still get dividends of companies if you hold them inside a mutual fund.

With dividends, there are three factors to consider, which I like to call the ABCs of dividends: Aristocrats, Burners and Calculations.

Aristocrats

Some companies hold themselves up to a high standard, and promise to provide dividends regularly. Aristocrats are dividend stocks that have consistently paid dividends every year to their investors for 25 years straight and include companies such as Coca-Cola and AT&T.

Burners

Companies that give dividends don't actually owe it to you—it's just a nice little bonus. So sometimes, if they burn through their money that year, they have nothing to offer their shareholders. In 2020, during the COVID pandemic, companies such as Estée Lauder and Ford Motors paused their usual dividends. The thing is, dividends come from the profit a company makes, so if profits are low or nonexistent, they may choose to not pay out to their shareholders—and there's nothing you can do about it. You have to be careful of burners; if you're trying to pay your mortgage with dividends, this can be a pain.

Calculations

It's important to not get sucked into the lure of some high-yield dividend offers and look at what is really being offered. Sometimes companies provide very high yields, which is the percentage you get in dividends for each share you have invested.

For example, if you owned $100 of stock A, and the dividend yield was 20 per cent, you'd get back $20 as a dividend. If you had $100 of Stock B, and the yield was 5 per cent, you'd get $5 as a dividend.

Stock A seems more attractive, if you just look at the dividend yield, but it may not be the best option. Let me tell you a little industry secret: those who speak the loudest have the most to hide.

A company that provides a wildly high dividend ('wildly high' is really anything that's above 6 per cent), is usually trying to lure investors into buying their shares because the company may be in trouble. An investor in training knows that if they're trying to invest for dividends, they are better off with stocks that give lower dividends but are more reliable than investing in companies that promise high dividends but go bankrupt in a few days.

It's also important to note not all companies give dividends; some companies may look at dividends as getting in the way of their growth. For example, imagine you are the CEO of a fast-growing electric car company. The company makes $1 billion in net income. Nice. You could distribute this to all your shareholders, or you could use this money to invest back into your company, investing in research, more engineers and bigger factories or machinery that can produce your cars faster. This in turn will make the company grow faster and increase the capital gains of its stock.

See, with dividends and capital gains, companies usually prefer to give you one or the other; they don't like to give you both. A company that needs to grow to give you that capital gain needs the money. A company like a bank or utility provider that gives you dividends is not interested in putting money into development, and they instead share their profits with you.

It's like a pendulum (see figure 6.1): when you invest in companies or funds, there is usually a dividend versus capital gain tradeoff.

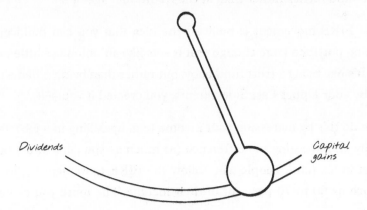

Dividends

Capital gains

Figure 6.1: dividends or capital gains

Blended funds (the forgotten Jonas brother of the stock market)

There is a third (not so well-known) way to make money in the stock market. It reminds me of the extra Jonas brother: there, but kind of forgotten about (sorry, Frankie). These are called blended funds, and they exist to fix this pendulum problem, aiming to get a healthy mixture of both capital gains and dividends.

Blended funds are picked to have a mixture of some growth companies that provide dividends, but also some companies that reinvest their dividends so they can continue to grow and create capital gains (and potentially even larger dividends later on). They're not as popular, but they serve as a good option for people still on the fence.

Starting a FIRE with our wealth

An extreme form of investing is starting to gain traction around the world. It's called financial independence, retire early (or FIRE), a concept coined in the 1992 bestseller *Your Money or Your Life* by Vicki

Robin and revitalised by Peter Adeney with his Mr. Money Mustache blog in the early 2000s. It's enabling people to retire earlier, in their thirties and forties rather than at the traditional age of 65.

The FIRE movement is built off the idea that you can build up an investing portfolio large enough that it acts like an unlimited little pot of gold. It's like being a trust fund baby, but rather than being gifted a trust fund by your Upper East Side parents, you created it yourself.

You do this by increasing your income (e.g. upskilling in a job), living frugally and investing the difference (as much as you can) into a broad market index fund. People who follow the FIRE movement try to save as much as 60 to 70 per cent of their income. The more you can save, the better.

Sounds too good to be true? I thought so as well, but the maths check out. The FIRE movement proposes that if you get your investing portfolio to the point where you can live off 4 per cent of its annual return you can retire from your job and work because you want to, not because you have to.

But won't 4 per cent every year drain your investment portfolio? This is where your financial knowledge comes in. Remember how I've said the stock market usually returns 7 to 10 per cent annually? Let's keep it at 7 per cent to be conservative. If, on average, the market rises at least 7 per cent annually, your draw down of only 4 per cent will still allow your portfolio at least 3 per cent to continue to grow. It's neat.

The first step is to decide how much you can live off. There are different levels of FIRE:

- **fat FIRE** is when the 4 per cent drawdown from your portfolio is at least $100 000 a year

- **lean FIRE** is when that drawdown is $25 000 to $35 000 a year

- **barista FIRE** is when the 4 per cent drawdown covers your basic expenses (such as mortgage and utilities) and you work part time to pay for any luxury you want to add to your life.

I know $35000 a year to live off doesn't sound like a lot, but if you think about it, if you were a single person who spent $500 a week on rent, $100 a week on food and $30 a week on utilities (heating, water, etc.) then your necessities are $32760 a year. This means you'd no longer have to work to survive, and any job you take on is for your own benefit.

There's one catch (because there always is). To live off $35000 a year by drawing down 4 per cent of a portfolio, that portfolio 'nest egg' that you save up will need to be *at least* $875000.

To live a leaner FIRE lifestyle, living off $20000 a year by drawing down 4 per cent, you'd need at least $500000 invested.

To live a life of fat FIRE, where you have an annual salary of $100000 a year, the nest egg gets much larger: at least $2.5 million.

I get it, $2.5 million sounds impossible. FIRE requires a level of privilege; you need to not only find a way to increase your income, but you also need to be able to decrease your living expenses. This gets significantly harder when you're a guardian or financially funding your parents' retirement, as many people of colour do, or if you have commitments to your family, such as contributing to a younger sibling's college fund. It also fails to take into account that not everyone has the ability to upskill, such as people living with disabilities, or those who are time poor due to family commitments.

With all that in mind, retiring even 5 or 10 years earlier, at 50 or 60, is still a feat, and something worth aiming towards if you can.

Even investing $500 a month, or $125 a week, for 37 years at a rate of 7 per cent annual returns can give you $1000000 (not adjusted for inflation). And if you are a student who may not be making much, you have time on your side, investing $62.50 a week for 46 years also brings you to $1 000 000.

★★★

Making money through the stock market can be broken into two main options: capital gains, which are suited for those interested in staying in the market for a long time, and dividends, for those who want to earn cash flow. Can't decide between the two? No worries, there's a flavour for that too: blended funds! At the end of the day, making money in the stock market is why you're here—so it's important to understand the different ways investors have been using it in their journey to financial freedom.

Actionable steps

1. Decide if you'd like to invest for FIRE, to retire early or for a lump sum for a goal.

2. Use an online FIRE calculator to work out the size of the investment portfolio you'd need in order to live on 4 per cent.

3. Decide if you'd prefer to be an investor for capital gains, dividends or a mixture.

Investor profile

NAME: Rita (pseudonym)

AGE: 30

JOB: Primary school teacher

1. What does your investment portfolio look like?

One property, 45 per cent in Smartshares US 500, 40 per cent Smartshares NZ Top 50, 10 per cent Pathfinder Global Water Fund, 5 per cent Pathfinder Global Responsibility Fund.

2. When did you begin investing and what was your first investment?

I began investing when I was working in retail back in 2010 where I first started KiwiSaver. I eventually bought a house in 2017 and in 2021 I bought my first share in an ETF 😊.

Other than KiwiSaver my first official investment was my own 3 bedroom home. I bought it for $225 000 in 2017 using the government housing grant, my KiwiSaver, my own savings, some money from my whānau (family), as well as money that my nana had left me that had matured over 13 years.

3. What stopped you from investing; were there any barriers you had to overcome?

I own my privilege as I have come from a loving, well-earning whānau and a great education. My only barrier in this case was in terms of buying shares in ETFs or other types of investments, I just had no idea where to even begin. I had no understanding with how it worked at all and felt scared/unsure of where to start.

4. What is the best piece of investing advice you've heard?

Don't sell when the market drops. Ride it out and stick at it for the long haul!

Part II

What type of investor are you?

7

Dancing stocks and risky numbers

Why the stock market moves and how to navigate risk

If you've ever paid any attention to stock market news, you know it can be extremely sensationalised. And that's coming from a stock market columnist herself! There are a lot of big words used to overcomplicate how the stock market is moving, and small dips of 1 or 2 per cent suddenly become 'looming crashes' with 'millions wiped out'.

The day of 12 March 2020 started off with a sunny morning. Before jumping out of bed, I checked my phone and scanned through the markets on my apps. It was three days after the US had declared travel bans due to the growing COVID-19 pandemic, when both the US stock market and the UK's FTSE 100 suffered from the greatest single-day percentage fall since the 1987 stock market crash. The Canadian S&P/ TSX had also dropped 12 per cent—its largest fall since 1940.

Still cosily wrapped up in my duvet, I dropped a bit more money into the S&P 500 and Tesla (which at the time wasn't part of the S&P 500 just yet) through an app on my phone. I always like to keep some cash ready for any drops. Then I got out of bed and got ready for work. I didn't realise it was the bottom of the market—that's impossible to tell until after the fact, anyway—and frankly I didn't care.

> *For a long-term investor, markets will go up and down, it's just what happens.*

The media, on the other hand, was having a field day: 'Global stock markets post biggest falls since 2008 financial crisis', 'Hundreds of billions wiped off values of indexes' and so on.

Let's talk about this. When news articles say things like 'hundreds of billions of dollars were wiped off the value of indexes', it sounds like many people must have lost their life savings, or at least a significant chunk of their money, during the drop. It sounds like people had to sell their homes to cover their losses and go live in their cars.

Yet the infamous 12 March 2020 crash saw the S&P 500 drop 9.5 per cent in a day. If you had a $100 000 portfolio in a well-diversified fund, you only lost $9500 in value. Someone with $100 000 to invest is not going to sweat over less than $10 000. What's more, that money wasn't 'wiped out'. Unless they panicked and sold their entire portfolio right then, they hadn't lost anything. These 'losses' would eventually recover once the market recovered. In this case, the market very quickly returned to pre-crash levels. In fact, some of the world's richest people saw their wealth double during the pandemic.

This hyper sensationalised perspective of market drops feeds into the curiosity and fear everyday people have about the stock market—and into the idea that it's risky and basically like gambling.

Why the market moves

The truth is that it's normal for markets to move. It's to be expected. There are 9.5 per cent drops from time to time. A market correction of around 10 per cent occurs every two years; a bear market, where the market falls 20 per cent, occurs about every seven years; and a crash of 30 per cent occurs every 12 years.

Let's take a step back. Why do stock prices dance around so much in the first place?

Have you ever looked at the movement of the market in a single day? Look at figure 7.1. What happened between 2 pm and 4 pm to cause that change in the stock price?

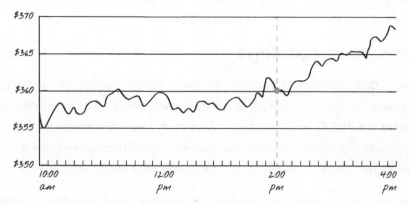

Figure 7.1: daily price movement of a stock

There are three main causes for stock and fund price fluctuations:

1. supply and demand

2. company earnings

3. investor sentiment.

Supply and demand

If you have 10 lollipops for $1 each, and 10 people want them, the lollipops will sell for $1. Simple enough. But if you had 10 lollipops and 100 people wanted them, people would start bidding higher for a lollipop. Naturally the price of the lollipop would rise, and keep rising until it reached the price the hungriest person was willing to pay.

If you had 10 lollipops for $1 each but only four people wanted them, the four people would likely be able to negotiate the price down with the seller, as there is more supply than demand. This is how stock prices change. They move by what we call 'market force'. There is a finite number of stocks that are available to purchase, and if more people want to buy a stock of Apple than the number of shares available, the price of Apple goes up; if fewer people want to buy than the numbers of shares outstanding, the share price goes down.

Company earnings

Every three months companies release a report, known as 'company earnings', to say how their company has performed. They release financial statements that show their balance sheet (their assets and debts), their cash flow (how money moves within the company) and their income (how much money they made, how much they spent and what the bottom line is).

Company earnings are a bit like a report card, and you, the investor, decide if it's satisfactory (see figure 7.2). Company earnings basically determine if investors pat themselves on the back and invest more into the company, or pull money out. Companies all release earning reports around the same time; they're called earning seasons (a bit like exam periods).

A long-term investor, however, isn't too fussed with earning season unless something fundamentally changes within a company. It can be confusing if a company performs well in its earnings report yet its stock price is dropping. After all, shouldn't the stock price go up if the company is doing well? This is the beauty of the market. What distinguishes a speculative investor from an investor in training is that the former will react to what's currently happening with the company, but the latter will react to the future outlook for the company. Rather than looking at company Y and thinking that if the value is going up currently it will continue to go up, investors in training take into account both the company's performance and its future outlook, with its announcements of new products or ventures.

Figure 7.2: company report card

For example, Meta saw a rise in company revenue from $28 billion to $33 billion—that's a feat during a pandemic, right? Yet Meta shares plummeted by 20 per cent the same day. Why? Well, in their 2022 earning report they announced that TikTok, a newer social media platform, was now serious competition to Meta. Investors reacted to the potential future of the company, not to its current state.

Investor sentiment

This is the overall attitude investors have towards a particular company or market. You could describe it as the gut feeling investors have about the market.

When investors feel optimistic about the market, they're said to display a 'bullish market sentiment'. And when they feel pessimistic, they display a 'bearish market sentiment'.

A bull market is one when stock prices are rising, and investors feel good. Overall, people are encouraged and happy to invest. It's like love is in the air, but for stocks. A bull market is defined as a moment when the market is up 20 per cent after two drops of 20 per cent, and it's named after the upwards motions bulls make when they fight.

A bear market is the opposite. It feels depressing. Stocks are down. Morale is low. People are scared and less likely to invest. It occurs when the entire market is down 20 per cent for at least a two-month period. Prices drop quickly. It's named after the downward swiping of their paws when bears fight. (Look, I don't really see it either. Let's move on.)

The macro factors of market movements

One of the best ways to avoid feeling uneasy during market fluctuations is to understand why markets are behaving the way they are. There are macro and micro factors (such as tax and regulations) that can cause a market to act the way it does. The most important to consider are these four macro factors:

1. economic growth

2. unemployment

3. inflation

4. high interest rates.

Economic growth

The overall health of the economy can affect the stock market. A good economy is where there is more spending: more people are going to malls and shopping. More people are going to restaurants and dining out. This leaves businesses with more revenue and hopefully more profit. Strong business growth then causes greater investor confidence and increases share prices.

Stocks that get affected by economic growth are known as cyclical stocks. These are stocks such as luxury resorts, hotels or aeroplanes; they do well when people want to spend money, and don't do so well when people are tight on money. 'Secular stocks', on the other hand, do well regardless of how the economy is doing. They're companies people need no matter what. The most common example is how people never stopped buying toilet paper, even during a pandemic.

Unemployment

Unemployment also affects the stock market. If there are more unemployed people, there is lower consumer spending and therefore reduced earning capacity for companies. However, there are still some stocks that perform well during high rates of unemployment. Consumer staples and defensive sectors (and no, I don't mean the army—I mean sectors that have stocks that provide dividends and earnings even in poor markets), as well as industries such as healthcare and utilities, are much better at weathering unemployment and recessions in general.

Inflation

We don't love inflation. Turns out, companies don't like it either.

Remember my lemonade stand from chapter 4? If there is high inflation, as an owner it now costs me more to buy lemons, cups and sugar. This means either I have to increase the price of my lemonade, which will decrease business as not everyone will want to pay $5 instead of $2 for a glass, or allow the increased costs to eat into my profit. This reduced earning capacity results in reduced stock prices for Sim's Lemonade Stand.

While my lemonade stand stock may be suffering, some stocks do well during inflation. Again, consumer staples, but also gold stocks, healthcare and material stocks benefit from inflation.

High interest rates

In 2020 and 2021, the US stock market rallied (which means it did really well) with a 16.26 per cent and 26.89 per cent return, respectively. One of the biggest contributors to this was that the Fed (the Federal Reserve Bank, which you can imagine as a group of people who decide the interest rates in the US, among other things), decided to drop interest rates significantly to stimulate economic growth. When you reduce interest rates, borrowing money suddenly gets 'cheaper' for people and businesses. This, in turn, encourages investing.

Changes in interest rates by the Fed take months, even sometimes a year after they're announced to go into effect, but funnily enough, the reaction from investors in the market is almost immediate.

High interest rates on the other hand mean borrowing money becomes more expensive. Companies must make higher payments for their business loans, and consumers have to spend more to pay off higher interest rates for mortgages, car loans and credit card debt. As a result, consumers spend less and companies make less. Which results in a drop in the stock price.

Stocks that do well with high interest rates are in the financial sector—banks, mortgage companies and insurance companies thrive. Remember, with higher interest rates on loans, the companies that provide the loans in the first place now get to ask for more money back.

A rule of thumb: you don't want to fight the Fed. If the Fed says interest rates are going up, the stock market usually takes a hit. When they say rates are going down, stocks jump back up.

Risky business

When it comes to the stock market it's important to understand the levels of risk involved. No investment type is completely risk free, not even a trusty blue-chip stock (those stable companies we all love, like Coca-Cola and Disney). The important thing about investing is aligning the risk of the types of investments to your personal risk tolerance (which you can work out with the quiz in 'Putting it all together'). It's all about doing what helps you sleep easier at night.

Risks based on macro and micro factors

There are a number of risks involved in investing:

- **market risk:** the risk that your stocks might drop in value due to something affecting the market, for example, shares fluctuating (equity risk) or interest rates fluctuating (interest risk) or the possibility of exchange rates changing (currency risk)

- **liquidity risk:** the risk that it's difficult to sell your shares when you want to

- **concentration risk:** accidentally keeping all your eggs in one basket (e.g. just owning airline stocks when COVID-19 hits)

- **credit risk/default risk:** the risk that the company you give money to (e.g. as a bond or if you lend money to a startup) can't pay you back

- **reinvestment risk:** if you reinvest the money you made with your original profits, but your profits now come at a lower rate (this usually happens with bonds)

- **inflation risk:** the risk of your investments not keeping up with inflation

- **horizon risk:** the risk that your investing goals change (e.g. losing a job and needing the money sooner)

- **longevity risk:** the risk of outliving your savings

- **foreign exchange risk:** the risk of investing in a country outside of your own; this covers currency risk, interest rate risk and political changes that may not affect your home country, but affect the country you're investing in.

Risk based on numbers

So how does one measure risk? There are a number of ways and calculations, but I'm going to give you the most common way since you're an investor in training.

If you see a company and you want to determine how volatile or risky it is compared to other stocks, I have a fairy godmother to help you. Her name is Beta.

Beta is a stock ratio that determines how risky or volatile a company is compared to others (see figure 7.3).

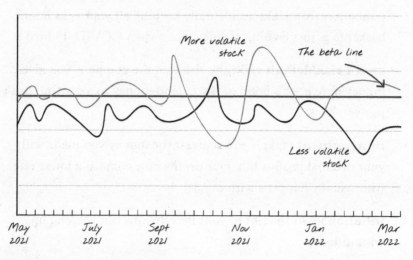

Figure 7.3: how beta works

Remember how we use the S&P 500 as the benchmark of what normal fluctuation is? We give the S&P 500 a beta of 1.

This is our benchmark: 1. Any stock or fund with a beta of:

- more than 1 is more volatile than the overall market

- less than 1 is less volatile than the overall market

- equal to 1 is just as volatile as the overall market.

So basically, if Tesla had a beta of 2, it is twice as volatile as the S&P 500. If the S&P 500 went up 10 per cent you'd expect Tesla stock to go up 20 per cent.

But if the S&P 500 dropped 9 per cent, you'd expect Tesla to drop 18 per cent. Higher risk higher reward, remember.

You can also use beta to compare two companies you may be weighing up (you can simply search for the companies' betas online rather than figuring out how to calculate it on your own). If you want the less risky option, you choose the one with the lower beta.

Risks based on timelines

Risk can also be assessed based on the amount of time you're planning to hold your investment portfolio.

Figure 7.4 (overleaf) is what the Russell 2000, an index filled with 2000 small-cap companies, looked like in one year: lots of ups and downs. If you started in Feb 2021, and needed the money a year later, you would have made a loss.

If you're investing for a longer period of time, the risk of losing money drops. Figure 7.5 (overleaf) shows the same fund over an 18-year period; those weekly/daily bumps in the market are smoothed out.

When it comes to investing in broad market index funds, the shorter the time frame you have to work with, the higher the risk. As a result, investors in training choose what they invest in based on their time frame.

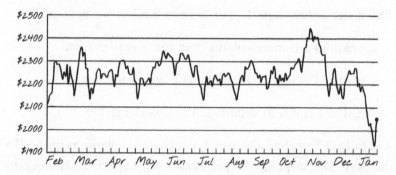

Figure 7.4: Russell 2000 from February 2021–February 2022
Source: Based on data from Yahoo Finance

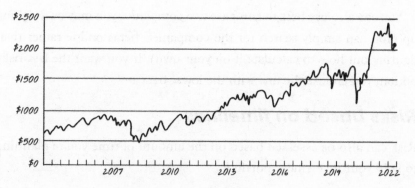

Figure 7.5: Russell 2000 from 2004–2022
Source: Based on data from Yahoo Finance

- **Investing for 1–3 years:** Choose cash or cash equivalents and bonds. Investors in training know that if they need the money in the next one to three years, they shouldn't put it in the stock market due to the short-term fluctuations.

- **Investing for 3–10 years:** Choose bonds and funds for diversification. Investors in training may choose a few individual stocks based on their risk tolerance.

- **Investing for 10–20-plus years:** Choose bonds, funds and individual stocks based on their risk tolerance. Investors in training investing over the long term have a portfolio that can handle some riskier investments (e.g. growth stocks) as time is 'more forgiving'.

***

One of the best ways to mitigate risk is by understanding your risk profile, because not all stocks and funds are created equally. Once you've decided what you're investing for and how long you're investing for, you can work backwards to decide what you want to invest in.

Risk is one factor to determine your approach to investing, but you can also apply different strategies, which are covered in the next three chapters.

Actionable steps

1. Research a company whose stock just dropped. See if you can find what caused the drop (e.g. bad earning report, poor future prospects, loss of investor confidence).

2. Research the economic growth, unemployment rate, inflation and interest rates (the macro factors) in your local economy.

3. Determine the timeline of how long you'd want to invest for.

Investor profile

NAME: Gloria (pseudonym)

AGE: 26

JOB: Secondary school teacher

SALARY: AU$77 474

1. What does your investment portfolio look like?

I have AU$67 000 invested in the ASX (93 per cent) and NASDAQ (7 per cent).

The ASX stocks are AEF 6.3 per cent, ARB 9.2 per cent, BHP 9.9 per cent, CBA 5.9 per cent, COL 2.5 per cent, CSL 12.7 per cent, NAB 11.7 per cent, NDQ 5.3 per cent, TCL 5.3 per cent, TLS 5.1 per cent, TPG 4.5 per cent, TUA 0.3 per cent, WES 8.1 per cent, WOW 6.5 per cent.

The NASDAQ stocks are Apple 3.5 per cent and Tesla 3.5 per cent.

2. How much and how often do you invest?

I save around $400 per month that I invest once I reach $5000 in my account, and I also reinvest my dividends.

3. Why do you invest?

I want to have financial freedom, and a large enough investment portfolio to earn a yearly salary of $50 000-plus without having to work.

4. Any tips for new investors?

Set a goal and start investing. If you are scared by the market then look at investing in safer stocks, such as banks and ETFs. The best time to start is now, but it's important to understand what risks you are willing to go for. What works for someone might not work for you. And just ask other people what they invest in.

8

The ethical investor

An investing strategy is something you determine as an investor in training to decide how you want to grow your money. It's like your skincare routine. There's some steps we all do, like washing our face, but some things that maybe other people do but you may not—like using retinol (but it's okay, you'll come around on the retinol). We'll be spending the next few chapters going over investing strategies. Pick up the strategies that interest you and park the ones that don't. You can always come back to these chapters to re-evaluate what your new strategy might look like.

Millennials and Gen Z have taken a different approach to investing than the generations before. We are more aware of the dangers of overconsumption, toxic ingredients and environmentally irresponsible practices. While we used to be blissfully unaware of where our purchases came from and how they were made, now companies are being called out for their unethical treatment of labour or environmentally harmful practices. In recent years there's been a complete 180; now we're questioning every form of consumption and demanding transparency.

We want to know what the ingredients on the back of our food packets mean. We want to know where and how our clothes are made. We want to know if our eggs were laid by hens with free access to the outdoors.

Our investments are no different. But how did the ethical investing movement begin?

Cigarettes and physicians

In 2010, an Australian oncologist (cancer doctor), Dr Bronwyn King, was meeting with a representative from her retirement fund. (In Australia this is called superannuation/super, in New Zealand it's KiwiSaver, in the US 401[k].)

The fund manager said Dr King's money was in the option of a balanced fund. Dr King picked up on the word 'option' and asked the manager to explain further. In this meeting she realised there were different funds available within her super, with different companies in them. Dr King also found out that out of the top five companies her retirement money was investing in, four of them were tobacco companies.

Let that last sentence just simmer for a moment. An oncologist, who spends every day of her job treating people for cancer, was unwittingly investing in one of the most common carcinogens in the world: tobacco. She owned a part in four tobacco companies! You can only imagine the shock and disgust she felt.

Most people would have just changed their fund and moved to another super, but Bronwyn went further. She wasn't okay with the lack of transparency around investments. She realised it was a worldwide issue and created an organisation, Tobacco Free Portfolios, that creates policies in Australia and in over 20 countries worldwide to reduce tobacco investing options, and to encourage more transparency around ethical investing.

Investing and having a moral compass can sometimes seem like they don't mix, but things have changed since 2010. In fact, investments in sustainable funds (which we'll get into shortly) more than doubled from 2019 to 2020. And in the US alone, over $17 trillion is under management using sustainable investing strategies. So, what are ethical investing, impact investing and socially responsible investing? Aren't they all the same thing? And how does one become an ethical investor?

Ethical investing

Ethical investing means investing in companies and funds based on your own values and morals. What may be ethical to you may not be ethical to someone else, and that's okay.

Ethical investing takes into account your religious, cultural, social and moral beliefs. It's very much like conscious consumer culture. In the same way that you'd rather buy a tote bag from a brand that you know pays fair wages, investors in training would rather invest in an ethical company over one that doesn't align with their values.

You basically get to decide if a company or fund meets your ethical standards, and you choose if you want to engage with them or not.

I need to stress that ethical investing is going to look different for different people. Someone may look at Tesla and invest in the company because they love the electric car movement and reducing dependence on oil, whereas another person may denounce Tesla's CEO for his beliefs or actions. Both investors are correct, because with ethical investing it is purely a personal decision.

It's putting your money where your mouth is, and only sharing your hard-earned money with the things that matter to you. Again, it's about doing whatever helps you sleep easier at night.

Socially responsible investing (SRI)

Socially responsible investing or SRI is very similar to ethical investing, but it goes one step further and focuses on investing in sustainable business practices. You get to choose or remove investments if you believe they do or don't adhere to sustainability guidelines. For example, you may choose to not invest in Nestlé as you don't believe in one company having a monopoly on an industry—that's an ethical choice. Someone else may not invest in Nestlé due to their past use of palm oil and its destruction of rainforests (which they stopped in 2021)—that is a sustainable choice.

An example of SRI investing is Environmental, Social and Governance (ESG) investing. This means companies you invest in focus on:

- **environmental issues,** such as climate change, water usage and pollution

- **social issues** surrounding health, safety and the treatment of employees

- **governance issues** surrounding management practices, business ethics or appropriate pay.

ESG investing is a common term used in the world of investing—if you ever see a fund with 'ESG' in its name you'll know they're trying to market themselves as an ethical option.

Its premise is based on investing in companies that have a positive impact on the world.

In recent times, more focus has been on companies that are environmentally conscious or help to fight climate change, either by reducing emissions or creating clean energy.

Impact investing

Impact investing is all about investing in companies or organisations that benefit society. For example, this is what the Bill & Melinda Gates Foundation does: they have invested over $60 billion in grants to companies like the Africa Health Fund, which improves the quality of healthcare in Africa, or Pfizer to create affordable contraception for the developing world.

How do you get into impact investing if you don't have a spare $60 billion?

You can be intentional with the change that you want to see and invest in companies that are executing this. Investors in training can be impact investors in their own right.

For example, you may be interested in supporting female-led companies, so look into ETFs such as SPDR® SSGA Gender Diversity Index ETF, which goes by the ticker 'SHE'. It's an ETF that provides exposure to (i.e. lets you in on) US companies that demonstrate greater gender diversity within senior leadership than other firms in their sector.

One thing to remember, however, is that when you invest in a company, your money doesn't go to them directly. But by investing in their shares, you can increase their stock price, which in turn shows them off as a stronger company and enables them to keep doing good work.

Ethical investments: woo-woo or cha-ching?

Ethical investing is a way to create change in the world and hopefully make money doing so. You don't necessarily have to sacrifice good returns for ethical investments.

Back in the day, ethical investing was seen as a bit 'woo-woo'. No-one really saw how you could care about the world's issues and try to make money at the same time.

However, times have changed. You no longer need to invest in tobacco, coal or casinos to make good returns. Morningstar, a well-respected global research agency, found that sustainable funds matched or beat returns across shares and bonds, both in the UK and overseas, over a 10-year period. The average annual return for a sustainable fund invested in large global companies has been 6.9 per cent a year, while traditional funds only brought in 6.3 per cent. (If you're thinking 'Hey! That's below the 7 per cent average return Sim has been mentioning', remember the average return of 7 to 10 per cent we've been working with is calculated over the past 40-plus years … it's always important to take into account what period of time you're dealing with.)

This better performance makes sense, though, doesn't it? Companies with better ESG practices will treat their customers and staff well. They'll have a better working environment. They'll have more loyal clients and care about the issues of today. They'll also have more diversity and, therefore, a greater breadth of decision-makers and change makers.

These are all characteristics of a company that is going to have greater productivity and greater financial success.

Of course *ethical investing is good for business*.

So how do you do it?

Wanting to invest in ethical companies and funds is one thing, but how do you actually go about doing this? There are a few strategies investors in training have under their belt. (The term 'strategy' may make it sound complex and maybe even a bit overwhelming, but don't worry—if this book has taught you anything, it's that the jargon in the investing world isn't nearly as scary as it seems.)

Positive screening

Positive screening is the simple act of choosing what causes matter to you and investing in companies that meet those criteria, such as:

- carbon neutrality

- Certified B Corps (companies that meet strict regulations and hold the highest standards for social and environmental performance)

- board or management diversity

- vegan friendliness

- support for nonprofits (e.g. a glasses company that has a 'buy one pair, we donate one pair' policy).

Any company or fund portfolio will show you whether they support causes important to you.

Negative screening

In 2016, many New Zealand retirement account holders learned that they were invested in companies making landmines and nuclear weapons. This of course outraged the general public and, as a result, most KiwiSaver funds now exclude warfare-related products from their portfolios. Making sure you don't invest in companies that don't align with certain ethical values is called negative screening.

Negative screening is a lot easier to measure as an investor in training. We tend to be clearer about what we don't like than what we do like

(I usually know what I don't want to eat over what I do). It's the idea of getting rid of investments in companies that engage with certain products or practices that you disagree with such as:

- gambling

- animal testing

- tobacco

- controversial weapons

- fur or leather

- palm oil

- adult entertainment.

What you want to negatively screen for will be different for most people, and that's fine. It's not about doing what others perceive as correct; it's about aligning your investments to your values.

ESG risk rating assessments

A third way to work out if something meets your ethical standards is through ESG risk rating assessments, which can be found on Morningstar.com. It's based off multiple exposure factors, such as business model, geography, financial strength and incident history. This provides an ESG risk rating as a number, with 0 to 9 being negligible and anything over 40 being a severe risk. Basically, if you're after ethical companies, you don't want the company you're investing in to have a high ESG risk rating.

What if you're invested in a fund that includes companies you don't agree with?

One of the issues with investing in an index fund or ETF is that you don't get to choose what companies are in there. For example, in early 2020 you may have invested in an S&P 500 ETF. Say you deeply dislike

Tesla. Later in the year Tesla becomes part of the S&P 500 and you face a moral dilemma—do you remove all your S&P 500 ETF shares?

The answer to this isn't clear cut, but you have a few options. You can choose to sell all your ETF shares. Or you can choose to keep your shares and invest in another ETF moving forward.

Some investors choose to keep the ETF if the company they don't like makes up a small percentage of that fund, and instead choose to not invest in that company's shares individually.

The biggest holding in the S&P 500 right now is Apple, and even that only makes up 7 per cent of the fund. Tesla in 2022 makes up 2 per cent of the fund. It's a decision for you to make if you decide that 2 per cent is important to you.

There are many ethical funds out there, but I'd like to give you two popular funds to start off with. (Be warned: their names are a mouthful.)

Vanguard FTSE Social Index Fund Admiral Shares (Ticker: VFTAX)

Don't let the name scare you. This is a fund that follows the S&P 500 index but negatively screens for ESG factors. It's important to note though that this fund still invests in Microsoft, Meta and Tesla, all of which might not meet some investors' criteria. It's a good reminder that what may be ethical to you may not be to someone else, and therefore checking the holdings of these ethical funds is important.

First Trust NASDAQ Clean Edge Smart Grid Infrastructure Index Fund (Ticker: GRID)

This ETF tracks the NASDAQ OMX Clean Edge Smart Grid Infrastructure Index, which invests in clean energy companies that are focused on electricity, such as Aptiv PLC or Johnson Controls International. It's heavily focused in one sector (clean energy), so there is lower diversification.

Is it actually ethical or is it greenwashing?

Unfortunately, you and I aren't the only two people who know that ethical investing has become more popular. Being tagged as ethical brings in more investors, and so funds are now more inclined to suggest their funds or companies are ethical or green as a marketing gimmick.

To make matters worse, there are no regulations to define what 'sustainable investments' involve—and the term 'ESG' can be slapped onto any fund. After all, ethical investing is so subjective, right?

An example of this is the BlackRock carbon ETF called BlackRock U.S. Carbon Transition Readiness ETF. (BlackRock is a famous investing management company.) This ETF is meant to follow the Russell 1000 and claims to have less than 50 per cent carbon intensity (which in simple terms is the amount of carbon dioxide it takes to make electricity). Sounds great for someone who wants to invest in clean energy, right?

However, after looking at their holdings, you'll realise the ETF invests in Chevron, which was partly responsible for spilling 77 million litres (17 million gallons) of petroleum and 18 billion kilos (18 million tonnes) of toxic waste in Ecuador. Not quite the environmentally friendly fund you may have had in mind.

It's important to not only be an ethical investor, but a vigilant one too.

Investors in training are aware that they cannot trust something to be ethical without researching it themselves and making their own judgements. Often, just by looking at a company's holdings, you'll see each company listed by its 'weight' in the fund, for example, FUND ABC is made up of:

- Apple: 10 per cent

- Google: 5 per cent

- Tesla: 4 per cent, etc.

If you're researching a fund, make sure you check out that fund's holdings to ensure they meet your criteria.

Investing and activism

As an investor you can vote for change with your money, pouring more into the issues and brands that you care about and actively choosing not to support companies that go against your beliefs.

It has never been easier for investors to get into the stock market, and it has also never been easier for groups of people to collectively stand together on issues they feel are important. Put them together and suddenly you've got a platform that corporations will listen to.

We can often feel helpless against large corporations, and they only seem to be getting bigger and more powerful. I'll let you in on a little secret, though. Companies only care about two groups of people: their customers and their shareholders. If you're not a customer boycotting the brand, you can be a potential shareholder who actively chooses to avoid or even sell their shares in protest. Companies do whatever they can to keep their shareholders happy; it is in their best interest, after all.

When large numbers of consumers start telling a company that they refuse to engage with them, or hold their shares, they start to listen. After all, it hurts their bottom line when there is less demand and their stock price drops—in the world of business, that is all that matters. Being an activist with your money has the benefit of hitting companies where it hurts the most. Unfortunately, companies are going to take more notice if you pull your shares out than if you stand in front of their office protesting.

I am all for marching and protesting for our rights and fighting for change, but I truly believe investing can be an important part of the overall conversation. Whether it's right or not, we live in a capitalist world, and money talks.

★★★

Investors in training know that ethical investing is an important part of their overall journey. It doesn't mean you need to run and invest in as many green-energy funds as you can, but rather that you get to choose investments that align with your morals and views.

No-one gets to have a say on what is right or wrong for your portfolio, except yourself. It's liberating to be able to choose what is important to you and to put your money into the changes you want to see in the world. Making money and making change in the world don't have to be mutually exclusive.

Actionable steps

1. Look into the retirement fund that you set up in chapter 4. What companies are included in your fund?

2. Note down three things you want to positively screen for in companies, e.g. diversity, carbon neutrality.

3. Note down three things you want to negatively screen for in companies, e.g. weapons, human trafficking, animal testing.

4. Research an ethical ETF that may spark your interest and see what companies they are 'holding'.

Investor profile

NAME: Lily (pseudonym)

AGE: 30

JOB: Marketing manager

SALARY: AU$150000 plus super

1. What does your investment portfolio look like?

AU$22000, all in ETFs: BetaShares Global Sustainability Leaders, 30 per cent; ASX 200, 30 per cent; NASDAQ 100, 30 per cent; iShares Global 100, 10 per cent; plus AU$60000 in super.

2. How much and how often do you invest?

I invest every month when I get paid, depending on what expenses I have. Minimum $1000 and maximum $2000.

3. Why do you invest?

To build long-term wealth. I have no plans to withdraw any funds in the next 10 years.

4. Any tips for new investors?

ETFs are a good entry to investing; they're a simple way to build diversification in stocks. Look for platforms that have low fees.

9

The female investor

When comparing those who identify as women and those who identify as men, in the stock market the average female investor makes more gains than men. They also lose less money than men. A 2021 Fidelity study analysed over 5 million investors and found that the women made 0.4 per cent better returns than the men. Now 0.4 per cent may not sound like a lot, but remember that beautiful concept of compound interest? These small gains compound over time.

This is also seen in the professional sphere: a 2021 study by Goldman Sachs (reported by *Forbes*) found that 48 per cent of female-managed hedge funds beat the market in 2020, while only 38 per cent of male-managed funds did the same. See figure 9.1 (overleaf).

While we are better investors, only four in 10 women investors are comfortable with their investing knowledge.

We're better investors when we do invest, but in general don't feel comfortable to begin investing. What is the gap?

It's a lack of knowledge. Specifically, a knowledge of investing strategies. Understanding what a stock or a bond is may be one half of the equation, but what about the strategies used by everyday female investors that give them a leg up? What are they doing differently?

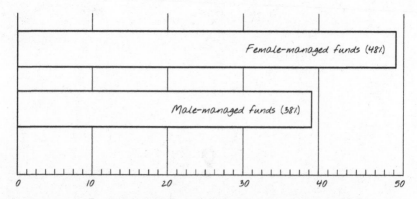

Figure 9.1: percentage of fund managers beating the market in 2021
Source: Based on data from a study by Goldman Sachs. Reported by Jacob Wolinsky. Here Is Why Female Hedge Fund Managers Outperform Men. 31 July 2021. *Forbes*

A lot of research has been done into this. In this chapter I'll get into the findings of that research, discussing the investing strategies women tend to use.

Women are told we're risk averse, but we're not. We're just risk aware.

Once we understand the risk and strategies involved in the world of investing, we're happy to dive in—we just need that foundational knowledge to begin with. If we know why we're better when we invest, we can start out on the right foot and have confidence that we're making the best decisions as investors in training.

One surprising thing is that many of these 'female-led' strategies are basically how the famous investor Warren Buffett invests. When Buffett was asked if he invested 'like a girl', Buffett replied: 'I plead guilty.'

Let's go through the seven investing strategies that have made female investors outperform their male counterparts consistently. This is how you 'invest like a girl':

1. passively invest

2. dollar cost average

3. emotions and the market

4. don't fall for FOMO

5. check your portfolios less

6. invest for the long term

7. invest in what you understand.

#1: Passively invest

You can try active investing: investing in individual stocks, where you try and pick companies that will beat the market. Or you can just invest in the market itself through a passive index fund. Female investors in general have shown a preference for the passive investing strategy. Let me tell you a secret: I know a female Wall Street trader who, while she actively trades professionally for her job, only personally invests in index funds. There are no stocks in individual companies in her personal portfolio. She knows trying to pick stocks is not worth her time, despite doing it for her full-time job.

We prefer to invest for the greatest gains with the minimum effort and involvement possible, which is where passive investing through index funds fits in perfectly.

With passive investing into index funds or ETFs, you end up diversifying your portfolio naturally as well. If you have even one share of the S&P 500, you're now a shareholder in 500 companies across a multitude of sectors in the US. By diversifying your risk, you're able to ride out the fluctuations in the market as well. For example, during the COVID-19 pandemic airline stocks dropped, but it wouldn't have mattered if you also had Zoom stocks, which went up. The even better part is that passive investors didn't have to rush to buy and sell once those Zoom or Microsoft shares started to soar; it was all adjusted automatically for them through their fund. That is the beauty of passive investing.

This is one of the few 'female' strategies that Warren Buffett doesn't use. Buffett is an active value investor; he tries to actively pick stocks that he thinks are undervalued. Basically, he's looking for Tatcha skincare at Nivea prices.

However, despite being an active investor, Warren Buffett is a huge advocate for the average person investing in index funds rather than trading. In fact, he believes that for everyday investors, active investing will only lead to 'worse than average results'. (Remember chapter 5 where I talked about his bet with a hedge fund that a passive index would beat the actively managed hedge fund's performance over 10 years?) When it comes to his family, he wants 90 per cent of his estate invested into index funds, specifically the S&P 500, when he passes away.

When you focus on passive investing you're looking at all the research that is stacked against you in terms of trying to pick winning stocks. Studies like those by the Research Affiliates in 2013 have found monkeys perform better in picking random stocks than investors. I can't say I'm any better at picking stocks than those monkeys.

#2: Dollar cost average instead of trying to time the market

Many people save up their first lump sum to invest and can't decide if they should put it all in at once or slowly over time. Should you wait for the market to drop?

Investors in training know that there is no point trying to time the market. If someone could perfectly time when the markets dropped and peaked, they would have become millionaires by now with their ability to always buy stocks at the bottom of the market and sell them when they knew the market was at its highest. But the reality is, you only know the bottom and the peak once they're gone, and by then it's too late.

Investors in training tend to know it's futile to try timing the market and instead use the strategy of dollar cost averaging. Let me explain this further.

How dollar cost averaging works

Imagine three friends. The first friend, Jacob, decided he wanted to save $200 a month and keep it in a high-yield savings account with a 3 per cent interest rate, saving it up to invest when the market drops. Let's say Jacob has been doing this over the last 40 years and ends up having the world's worst timing. In fact, he invests the day before all of the four big crashes, meaning he makes an immediate loss the day after he puts his money in ... four times. Poor Jacob.

But let's say Jacob has some sense in him, and he doesn't panic-sell and instead holds on to his investments. By the end of the 40-year period he'll have made $663 594.

Then there's Afia. Afia is like Jacob and wants to time the market. She also saves $200 a month and keeps it in a high-yield (3 per cent) savings account. She ends up having the best timing in the market and somehow ends up investing in the lowest point of the four biggest crashes.

Afia ends up with a portfolio worth $956 838.

Now there is a third friend, Nina. She decides to not worry about timing the market and simply invests $200 every month into the same fund, through all the highs and lows.

Nina ends up with $1.38 million at the end of 40 years. How? It's the beauty of dollar cost averaging: that you ride out the highs and lows of the market, and you reap the rewards of compound interest. See figure 9.2 (overleaf) for a graph of all three different investment approaches.

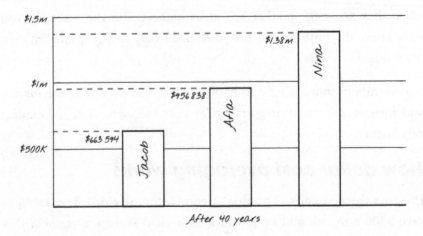

Figure 9.2: Jacob's, Afia's and Nina's investments

Some days you'll invest in the funds when they're a bit higher, some days you'll invest in funds when they're slightly lower, but by averaging out your chances of investing at a 'good price', you end up doing better in the long term.

The thing with the stock market is that a lot of big gains in the market can be concentrated in a few days; the market doesn't go up the same percentage every day. The Bank of America analysed data from over 91 years, all the way back to 1930, and found that there were only 10 days each decade that made a huge difference to an investor's portfolio. In fact, if an investor had missed out on the S&P 500's 10 best days each decade, their total return would be 28 per cent lower. But if they bought and held their investments through the ups and downs instead of trying to time the market, their return over the 91 years would have been around 15 000 per cent. They also found that some of the best days in the market actually follow big drops, as seen in the COVID-19 crash, where stocks rallied (a jargon term which means 'rose upwards') significantly.

No-one can time the market. Investors in training dollar cost average and keep some cash, perhaps $1000 to $2000, aside just in case they see a drop and want to add extra money into their fund. But that's their extent of 'trying to time the market'.

Time is money, and investors in training would rather spend their time enjoying their lives and having meaningful experiences than hunching over a screen daily trying to work out the next drop. After all, aren't we investing for more freedom of time?

You can dollar cost average every week, fortnight or month. If you are unsure which timeframe is better, the rule of thumb is that the more money you have to invest the more often you can invest to counteract the brokerage fees you might face at each investment. Investing $10 a week with a $2 fee may not be wise, but investing $500 a week for a $2 fee suddenly isn't so bad.

Another downside of trying to time the market is that sometimes people get so much analysis paralysis they miss out on the market completely.

You don't want to be the person who keeps waiting for the best time to invest and ends up never investing at all.

#3: Emotions and the market

One of our top traits is that we have good emotional control when the markets fluctuate. (A bit ironic since we've always been told that we're an overly emotional gender and any bad mood is due to probably being 'on our periods'. I guess our investing portfolios say otherwise.)

You know those stock photos of men with their heads in their hands during stock market news? You do not want to react like those men during volatile times in the market, because you know as an investor in training that volatility is to be expected and that you're investing for the long term. Bet they feel really silly now.

When emotions take over our strategy, investors tend to elevate risks that they could otherwise avoid. This is not exactly brand-new information; we all know you don't make the best decisions when your judgement is clouded by emotions.

Having emotional discipline during a bear market isn't easy for anyone. It takes guts to look at your stocks 'all in red' and not want to panic and pull your money out. Remember, if you have 10 shares, even if they're in the red, you still have 10 shares. The number of shares you have during a market downturn hasn't changed, it's just the value of them that's changed, and, if you invest in a diversified low-cost broad market fund, you should eventually see the value rise back up.

Instead, when the market drops, investors in training with good emotional control see it as an opportunity to buy more stocks they love—it's a sale day for your favourite stocks and funds. Like seeing that MacBook you wanted, but it's now $999 instead of $1999. (It's important to note that you don't want to just buy any falling stocks during market drops. How many times have you regretted impulse buying something you didn't need just because it was a 'good deal'?)

The other side of the emotional coin is being overconfident when the stock market is doing well. There's a saying in the investing world that a rising tide lifts all boats. When the market itself is doing well, like what we experienced in late 2020 to late 2021, you could take a punt at a few companies and see them rise in value. Investors in training know not to mistake good luck or good timing as skill. They also know not to over-invest in a recent winner. If their Microsoft stock went up 200 per cent, it doesn't mean they should necessarily invest more money into it. It's still important to stick to the fundamentals of analysing the company's future growth. One of the worst mistakes an investor in training can make is selling what has done poorly and putting more money into what has done well. (That's buying high and selling low, the opposite of what you're supposed to do!)

One of Warren Buffett's famous quotes is to be greedy when others are fearful and fearful when others are greedy. He's essentially saying to invest in the opposite way from what your emotions are telling you. It's not an easy skill to learn, but investors in training will be rewarded for their ability to strengthen their emotional discipline.

#4: Don't fall for FOMO — stick to a strategy

Fear of missing out (or FOMO) investing is when investors feel pressured to invest in a company or fund because they are scared they'll miss out on a big opportunity.

No-one wants to be left behind in a gold rush. No-one wants to be the person who laughed at Bill Gates when he shared his views about how the internet would change the world. Everyone wants to find the next Apple: stocks that skyrocket after their IPO and make many people wealthy.

However, for every Apple there are hundreds of stocks that don't make it. After all, small-cap stocks, smaller companies looking to grow quickly, are often more volatile.

Now that it's easier and faster to access information than ever before, FOMO investing is harder to resist, especially with the likes of GameStop or AMC skyrocketing in 2021. GameStop was a videogame and merchandise retailer that was on a downward trend. Yet, due to FOMO investing and a concerted effort by investors on Reddit's r/wallstreetbets forum to 'stick it to the man' the stock went from US$17.69 on 8 January 2021 to US$325 on 29 January... and then down to US$40.59 on 19 February (see figure 9.3, overleaf).

Seeing friends and family have success with a particular stock can provide investors with an overly heightened sense of confidence about the investment.

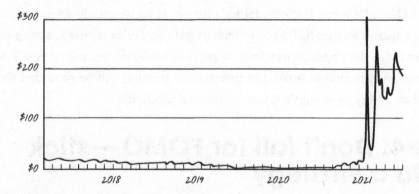

Figure 9.3: GameStop's wild ride
Source: Based on data source from GameStop - Stock Price History |
GME. Macrotrends LLC.

A recent New Zealand study by the Financial Markets Authority (FMA) found 31 per cent of investors in 2020 and 2021 had bought stocks on the basis of FOMO, and that 27 per cent invested based on a recommendation from someone they know, without doing their own research. They didn't want to miss out and jumped on the investment. The FMA were alarmed to say the least, and started a country-wide campaign to educate investors about the dangers of FOMO investing.

> *Female investors are less likely to succumb to peer pressure in investing and are more likely to hold on to their investing strategy.*

They realise the importance of blocking out the noise and sticking to their strategy of dollar cost averaging into their index funds, and keeping speculative investing, like with FOMO stocks, to a bare minimum.

This is not to say female investors do not engage with FOMO investing. The study found that of their sample speculative investors, those who were strongly influenced by FOMO investing, 66 per cent were males and 35 per cent were women.

It would be unrealistic to think that investors aren't going to be tempted by FOMO investing throughout their entire investing journey, so if you are going to do it, only put in what you are comfortable with losing. Investors in training know that they should keep any speculative stocks as a small percentage of their portfolio—ideally less than 5 per cent.

One investor, gender unknown, from the study stated 'how tempted I was to jump on the bandwagon, as a lot of my friends did. But the result' (once the FOMO stock dropped) 'just reiterated to me how I'm only here to play the long game, and these short sharp rises are synonymous with lottery winnings'.

As the Securities and Exchange Commission (SEC) in the US warned in 2017, 'it is never a good idea to make an investment decision just because someone says a product or service is a good investment'. Say less, SEC.

#5: Check your portfolios less frequently

Female investors spend more time researching stock picks, but once we do, we don't check them as often. Nearly half of investors check their stock performance at least once a day, and that's worrying. You do not want to be checking your portfolio too often.

Why? As we've learned from money psychology, we hate losing money more than we love making money. We're more upset if we lose a $100 note than we are excited when we find a $100 note. Even though the value we lose or gain is the same, the emotional output differs a lot. We feel the pain of loss about two times more intensely than we feel the pleasure of gain. It's a concept called loss aversion, discussed by Daniel Kahneman and Amos Tversky in their 1984 study 'Choices, Values, and Frames', then later in Kahneman's book *Thinking, Fast and Slow*.

The relationship between how often you check your portfolio and how much money you make is documented well; the more often you check your portfolio, the more likely you are to see a loss.

An investor who checks their stocks more often, for example daily instead of quarterly, has an increased risk of losing more money, Kahneman observed. You're more likely to act on what you see.

This is one of the key strategies to having a successful investing portfolio. How often should one check their portfolio? Technically, as little as possible. Investors in training usually check their portfolio once every month to once every quarter. If you're currently checking daily, start off with monthly to get into the habit of checking it less, and then eventually move this to quarterly.

This doesn't mean only invest once a month or once a quarter, but have automatic systems set up that invest for you, so that you don't have to check your stocks as often.

Investing information has never been more accessible, but that doesn't mean investors should constantly access it. Female investors are able to control this urge to stay updated on the small movements of their portfolios and end up being better off for it.

#6: Invest for the long term; don't trade as often

Female investors increase their earnings by trading (i.e. buying and selling) less frequently. Men are 35 per cent more likely to trade stocks than women.

During periods when there is a lot of volatility in the world, such as during presidential elections, ebola outbreaks or a debt crisis, the number of trades on platforms increase — however, women continue to trade less frequently than men.

Even more recently, during the 2020 COVID-19 pandemic, women traded less during the market turmoil than men, leaving them better off in the long term. Nutmeg, an investing broker, found that during the start of the pandemic in March 2020, men were twice as likely than women to withdraw money during the downturn of the market, solidifying their losses. Whereas 95 per cent of women made no adjustments to their portfolio.

There's a popular phrase in the world of investing called 'buy and hold', and it's popular for a reason.

Female investors tend to invest for the long term and don't change their investing strategy easily. It's easy to get affected by the hype of FOMO or fear when the market drops, as mentioned earlier. But investors in training know that, on average, the stock market returns 7 to 10 per cent, and if anything is suggesting a guaranteed return of more than this, it is unlikely to be true. They are also aware that if they have a solid investing strategy that includes diversifying in broad market funds, buying and holding and checking their portfolios less frequently, there's less to worry about. It goes back to the idea of starting out with a solid foundation based on knowledge and research. Investors in training know that a house will crumble if it doesn't start out with good foundations.

When it comes to marital status, the pattern is still the same: according to a Wells Fargo report in 2019 'Women & Investing', single women trade 27 per cent less frequently than single men. Interestingly enough, men's trading activities quieten down when they begin sharing finances with a female partner.

This tendency to buy and hold could be attributed to female investors being more risk aware, and therefore deciding to engage in further research before investing. Female investors are also more likely to seek financial help (a bit like the stereotype of women being more likely to ask for directions when lost) if they have queries.

A study led by the Haas School of Business and UC Davis Graduate School of Management found male investors tend to be more overconfident in their investments, which leads to more frequent trading, and therefore lower returns.

Investors in training, regardless of what gender they identify with, can learn from these behaviours and understand the importance of trading less frequently and seeking advice if they are unsure.

#7: Invest in what you understand and ignore the rest

The final strategy that female investors employ is being honest with themselves and only investing in what they understand. This is not to say male investors understand more — but if both groups are equally ignorant about a new investment class, male investors are still more willing to try it out than female investors.

For example, female investors will invest in assets such as crypto-currencies, but on a lower scale and keep it to a smaller percentage of their overall portfolio.

It's a concept that Warren Buffett himself employs; he openly admits that he doesn't invest in many tech companies because he does not understand them. While this may have kept him out of some big gains from tech booms, it has also protected him from the Dotcom Bubble in the early 2000s (mentioned in chapter 2), where people were investing in any company with '.com' in its name.

Five rules of investing like a girl

When researching companies to invest in, there are five rules to employ to help you invest 'like a girl' (or like Warren Buffett), as outlined in table 9.1.

Table 9.1: Five rules of investing like a girl

Rule	Reasoning	Example
Company has a moat	This makes sure that the company is well known or has a patent that stops competitors from trying to take its business	Coca-Cola
Company invests in research	More important for younger investors; you want a company that is continuing to innovate and grow	Pfizer
Company has good leadership	A company that has good leadership is more likely to have a trickle-down effect on the growth of the company and how it handles downfalls	Alphabet (Google)
Company is adaptable	Companies that respond well to change don't get left behind, like Nokia during the smart phone revolution	Apple
Company has a growing bottom line	A company that has an increase in revenue isn't very helpful if their net income or bottom line isn't growing as well	Microsoft

***

The strategies employed by these investors show an investor who is calm, collected and confident in their stance. They don't trade as often, don't check their portfolio as often and don't waiver under pressure to join the hype.

It is easy to be swayed by the news but an investor in training is sure in themselves and agile enough to ask for help when they need it.

Actionable steps

1. If you have begun investing, circle the strategies that you are already employing and note down which ones you want to start doing.

2. Decide how often you want to review your investments— monthly or quarterly—and stick a date in your calendar. Don't check your investments until the date comes.

3. Choose a company at random and see if it fits the 5 rules of investing like a girl.

Investor profile

NAME: Jamie (pseudonym)

AGE: 27

JOB: Business owner and professional basketball player

1. What does your portfolio look like?

5 per cent in US Real Estate VNQ, 11 per cent Emerging Markets Stock ESGE, 34 per cent Developed Markets Stock ESGD, 39 per cent US Stocks SUSA, 3 per cent US Bonds BND, 3 per cent Global Bonds BNDX, 5 per cent Bitcoin

2. When did you begin investing?

February 2021 with $500 USD in the Bumble IPO. Why? Youngest female CEO to take a company public, with her son on her hip, feminist dating app, putting the power in the hands of women, need I say more?

3. What stopped you from investing; were there any barriers you had to overcome?

The investing community seemed so unapproachable for me, too difficult to understand, and living in Jordan trying to find ways to invest made it even more difficult.

4. Any tips for new investors?

When you invest, it's like hiring your money as your employee and the money's job is to create more money for you.

10

The lazy investor

By now you understand the difference between active and passive investors. Active investors are trying to beat the market average by choosing stocks, putting time and energy into reading company financial statements, skimming through balance sheets, looking at a company's assets and debt and reviewing how the company controls its cash flow.

Some active investors can beat the market in the short term but this gets harder as time goes on, and for long-term investors—those who are investing for 10-plus years—they're better off taking the passive approach, or at least keeping some of their portfolio in a passive strategy. In this chapter we'll get into the lazy (i.e. passive) investor strategy, but first, let's look into how active investors do what they do.

Active investors

Active investing can be broken down into two approaches: fundamental analysis and technical analysis.

Fundamental analysis

Fundamental analysis is the practice of trying to work out the intrinsic value of a stock because you believe the intrinsic value is different to its actual value. You look at the book value of companies and analyse tables to see if it's worth your time. It's the process Warren Buffett uses to determine if he will invest in a company or not.

My mum practises fundamental analysis when we travel to India by only paying what she believes something is worth at markets. In the process of haggling, if she believes something is worth 100 rupees and the shopkeeper is trying to sell it for 150, she'll walk away. She doesn't see the price of an item and assume the price equals its value.

Meanwhile, my father would just pay the 150 rupees. He believes the cost of an item is already reflected in the price. This is what passive investors do. They do not believe the intrinsic value of a stock or fund is separate, they believe all factors that could affect the stock have been 'priced in' to the stock price.

There are many ways to find out the 'intrinsic value' and compare it to its current price. The discounted cash flow method (DCF) is the most popular. It tries to work out the value based on projections of how much the company will generate in the future.

The calculation for this is:

$$DCF = \frac{CF_1}{1 + r^1} + \frac{CF_2}{1 + r^2} + \frac{CF_n}{1 + r_n}$$

where:

- *CF* is the cash flow for the given year

- CF_1 is for year one

- CF_2 is for year two

- CF_n is for additional years

- r is for the discount rate.

However, it's much easier to plug this into any online calculator.

Active investors believe that, sometimes, if a company's price drops (e.g. after bad news) it's only a temporary drop and therefore they can purchase the stock on sale. Let's say you want to invest in Boeing after some bad news about the company came out, and you believe that it has temporarily dropped in price.

The stock price is $200 but the DCF method shows you the intrinsic value is $210. This means you've found a company on 'sale' so you purchase it, knowing you've scored yourself a bargain.

Technical analysis

Technical analysis, on the other hand, takes an active investing strategy that looks at graphs rather than tables, and also, like a passive investor, assumes the stock price has been priced in; that is, that the value of the stock is equal to its price. They believe that history can be used to assess how stocks perform and people (and therefore the supply and demand of the market) behave. They believe you can use patterns to determine what the next move is.

These are the types of investors you've always been intimidated by, the ones with 'candle stick charts' (see figure 10.1, overleaf).

There are hundreds of patterns that technical analysts use to forecast how a stock will move, including trendlines, channels and momentum indicators. Critics believe that technical analysis only works at times and that history doesn't repeat itself. It can also be a bit of a self-fulfilling prophecy; for example, when technical analysis 'predicts' correctly, then credit may be given to the strategy, but if it doesn't go to plan, the blame may be given to the analyst who 'just understood it wrong'.

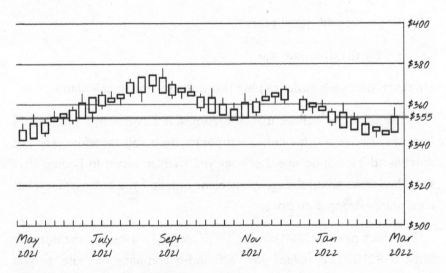

Figure 10.1: a candle stick chart

The lazy investor

The data seems to back the critics of active investing. Between 2004 and 2014, Morningstar compared over 500 actively managed funds in the US with passively managed funds. The active funds returned 8.05 per cent and the passive funds returned 9.27 per cent. Investors in training don't see the benefit of greater work for lower outcomes, and thus the lazy investor was born.

Before we begin, the term 'lazy investor' is not a dig at this strategy. It's just referring to how easy it is to use. The lazy investor, or three fund portfolio, is an investing strategy coined by John Bogle, the guy who invented index funds. Those who are huge fans of the method are self-proclaimed 'Bogleheads'.

In the personal finance community this investing portfolio is regarded as the gold standard of how to allocate assets if investors in training are unsure of where to begin. It's an easy-to-understand and popular risk management tool.

Index funds or ETFs (remember the baskets that invest into a list like the S&P 500 or the FTSE 100) are an integral part of the lazy investor strategy. It works by holding a total of three ETFs.

I like to think of it as picking a group of friends; each fund represents a type of person you want in your friendship group. You adjust the percentage of each friend type you'd prefer to suit your personal needs, and this is going to change over time. The people you like to hang out with at 15 aren't always the people you want to have at 20 or 30 as you grow and develop.

The three funds that a lazy portfolio has are:

1. a broad US market index ETF

2. a broad international market index ETF

3. a bond ETF.

Why a broad US market index fund?

This is funds such as the Vanguard 500 Index Fund ETF (VOO) or Vanguard Total Stock Market Index Fund ETF (VTI). They allow investors to have access to either the top 500 companies in the US or the entire US stock market respectively.

Why the US market? It holds some of the world's largest companies, holding 55.9 per cent of the market share of the total world equity market. You can replace this with the index in your home country such as the FTSE 100 in the UK, the ASX 200 in Australia or the NIFTY 100 in India. But with the US market, you get more exposure to some of the biggest brands on the planet. It's like having a friend that's a big shot—they're popular and they're not too risky to be around, but sometimes they do get overly confident so they aren't entirely free of risk.

Why a broad international market index?

An example of one of these is the Vanguard Total World Stock Index Fund ETF. This is your worldly friend. They open you up to international experiences. This fund has over 7000 stocks from 47 countries. It invests in both foreign and US stocks by tracking the FTSE Global All Cap Index, which covers countries from both developed and emerging markets. The US accounts for 59 per cent of this fund followed by countries like Japan, UK, China, Canada, France, Switzerland and Germany, which make up the rest.

The benefit of this ETF is that you are invested in every sector in every part of the world. The diversification is strong.

It's important to note that this friend is slightly more volatile due to their jet-setting ways; they might get stuck somewhere due to a railway strike or regime change.

Emerging markets aren't as stable as the US market, but that doesn't mean they shouldn't be a part of the gang.

Why a bond ETF?

If stocks are the risk-taking, more extroverted friends, then bonds are the introverts. And in every group of friends you need the loud to be balanced out with the quiet—trust me.

A bond ETF such as the Vanguard Total Bond Market Index Fund ETF is an option to consider. It tracks the Bloomberg Aggregate Float-Adjusted Bond Index. The benefit of having bonds in your portfolio is that it reduces risk, even if it comes with a slightly lower reward. You're able to have a bit more diversification in the market. When you're hungover and have lost your wallet, stranded somewhere after a big night out with the extroverts, the bond ETF is there to pick you up and give you a cup of tea.

They're the friends you don't really realise you need until things turn to poop.

Why have all the examples been Vanguard related?

Vanguard host the lowest fees. A lot of passive funds are very similar, and often invest in the exact same things. That only leaves one feature to compare, and that's fees. By all means feel free to invest in other branded ETFs—you'll get the same returns, the fees will just be different.

How to balance your friend group

So what per cent of each fund do you need in your portfolio? Let's work it out.

This is going to be different for each person, but a rule of thumb is that the riskier you are willing to be, the more stocks, like the US and international index funds, you're going to have in your portfolio, with a lower percentage of bonds (see figure 10.2).

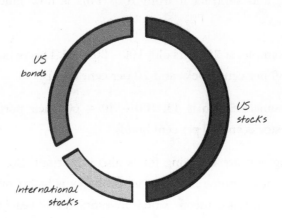

Figure 10.2: riskier lazy investor

Someone who doesn't want any friendship drama, and instead wants less risk for less reward, would consider a portfolio that is more bond heavy (see figure 10.3).

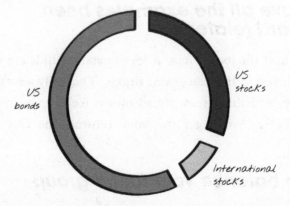

Figure 10.3: less risky lazy investor

But how do you decide what your risk profile is? Think about two things:

1. how old you are

2. how long you want to invest for.

A rough way to work this out as a lazy investor is to take the decade of your age and subtract it from 100. This is how much should go towards stocks.

So, for example, at 25 years old, 100 – 20 = 80. This person's portfolio should be 80 per cent stocks and 20 per cent bonds.

But for someone who is 45, 100 – 40 = 60; their portfolio may be 60 per cent stocks and 40 per cent bonds.

How long you are investing for is also important. Someone who is investing to buy a home in five years probably is better off being more bond heavy, whereas someone who is investing for 20 years to retire early could get away with more stocks than bonds, as they have more room to ride out the waves. You can also take the quiz in 'Putting it all together' to work out your personal risk profile.

So why the three fund method?

The advantages of this approach are:

- it's an easy set-and-forget method

- you can adjust your risk level

- it offers high diversification for low fees.

It's an easy set-and-forget method

The lazy investor portfolio is a great way to begin without having to do a lot of research and spend a lot of time going through data. Rather than trying to beat the market, John Bogle believed in being the market. If you can't beat 'em, join 'em.

If you automate your finances so that X amount of your pay cheque goes into an account, and every month a set dollar amount goes into your online brokerage account, which splits your money across these three investment funds, you have created an automatic system that you do not need to check. You do not need to worry about timing the market or missing out on good deals. It is truly a set-and-forget method.

You can adjust your risk level

One of the best parts about this method is the ability to adjust it against horizon risk, which you may remember is the risk that you have a change in your life and suddenly need to adjust your strategy.

If I need my money sooner, let me invest into more bonds.

If I decide I don't want to buy a home anymore and this money is going to be my retirement fund? Let me buy more stocks.

The ease of changing your position without buying and selling hundreds of stocks is one of the beauties of the lazy investor method.

It offers high diversification for low fees

Many online brokerages charge a fee for every company you invest in. This can usually range from a few cents up to $15 if you're unlucky. If you were gaining access to 7500 companies by investing in each of them on their own, your brokerage would have a champagne party using the money from your brokerage fees alone.

By investing in funds, you lower the fees you must pay for the number of companies you are exposed to. Index funds and ETFs also have lower fees in general, with Vanguard ETF fees being as low as 0.03 or 0.04 per cent at times.

Downsides to the lazy investor

That's not to say there aren't a few downsides to the lazy investor strategy: you can't tailor your investments to your ethics, and you're only getting average returns.

Can't always be ethical

With the lazy investor method you are investing in a wide range of companies across the world, which also means being exposed to certain companies you might prefer to avoid, such as Johnson & Johnson or Nestlé. Some investors in training are okay with these companies receiving such a small percentage of their asset allocation, but some investors may not be as comfortable.

It is entirely possible to swap out ETFs in your lazy portfolio for ones that align with your ethics, but also make sure they have a broad range of companies in them. For example, an ETF with 100 companies is better in terms of diversification than one with only 30.

You're getting average returns

If you make simple portfolio choices that invest in the market instead of trying to beat the market, you're spending less time worrying. But this also means you're just getting average returns.

For some people, being average isn't enough. The investor in training understands a 7 to 10 per cent annual return over the long term is a good average to aim for, but they may be enticed by other investors who make 20 or even 30 per cent returns in the short term through stock selection.

***

The most important thing is for investors in training to be comfortable with their investing strategy and to stick to it. It is easy to be swayed, and to question what you are doing when you see other investors behave in reaction to the market, but not everything that glitters is gold.

Actionable steps

1. Determine if you'd prefer to be a passive investor, fundamental investor or technical investor.

2. Try out a DCF intrinsic calculator online to test whether a stock you think is undervalued (on sale) is actually undervalued.

3. If you're a passive investor, determine the percentage you'd want in stocks versus bonds.

Investor profile

NAME: Nicky (pseudonym)

AGE: 30

JOB: Software engineer

SALARY: US$300 000

1. What does your investment portfolio look like?

US$400 000 in a simple three-fund portfolio: VTSAX (49 per cent), VTIAX (21 per cent), VBTLX (25 per cent). This is in addition to my retirement accounts and company RSUs (restricted stock units). Trying to actively sell my RSUs to reduce the proportion of single stock in my portfolio but it's hard because of the capital gains accrued.

2. How much and how often do you invest?

On average $3000 monthly.

3. Why do you invest?

So I can have more control of my time in the future. I want to live a FI (Financially independent) life when I don't 'have to' work for money anymore.

4. Any tips for new investors?

Keep it simple: instead of investing in ad hoc single company stocks, try to have a well-balanced portfolio with asset allocation according to your age.

Make sure you are using all the tax advantaged accounts you can. Not only your 401(k)s, but also the IRAs and the after tax accounts ('Megabackdoor'). Power of compounding along with no taxes on growth makes a big big difference in how much your money grows over a period of time. They should teach this in school!

(Especially for young girls) investing and money can sometimes be taboo topics. It might seem superficial to talk about money. There is a study that women are more comfortable talking about their weight than about their money. We need to get over this. Good finances lead to freedom—freedom to spend your time the way you want and lead a life you want. It is an essential life skill.

11

Spicy investing

Day trading, forex, options, crypto and NFTs...I call them spicy trading as they don't fall under the rules of long-term investing, but they can still have space in an investor's portfolio under the section of speculative investments. Every responsible financial book will tell you to abstain from these, but this one will tell you that if you're going to try it (which you probably are), at least have all the facts and be safe.

There are a few assets that you can invest or speculate into, many of which you will probably learn about through social media. That doesn't mean to say they're all scams, but this chapter is going to cut through the noise and explain exactly what is involved, how you might possibly make money and how to actually invest in these 'spicier' assets.

Day trading

Day trading is the idea of buying a stock and selling it within a 24-hour period. Remember how stocks can fluctuate within a single day? Day traders attempt to take advantage of this market movement and buy stocks at lower prices and then sell them quickly. This requires being vigilant, often using day trading software to watch the movement of the market. It falls within the realm of what we used to assume investing looked like—someone staring at multiple screens with lots of graphs.

Day trading is buying into a stock when it is $5 at 10 am and then selling it when it is $11 at 12 pm. You end up profiting $6, and then you take that $6 and keep going with the hope that you keep adding more money and snowballing your profits.

Investors in training know that day trading may be a short-term option, but professional traders recommend never putting more than 1 per cent of your portfolio into a single trade due to the high level of risk involved.

Day trading isn't lucrative by any stretch of the imagination. Up to 95 per cent of traders fail to make a profit. It also requires a large amount of capital (money) to begin with.

The Financial Industry Regulatory Authority (FINRA) in the US recommends that day traders keep a fund of at least US$25 000 in their account at a minimum. This is to protect investors from getting too over-leveraged (borrowing too much money to invest) and so they have enough in their accounts to weather the downfalls during trading.

While it might look exciting, and can come with big wins, most often it does not. Investors in training know that the wealthiest investors in the world grew their money through buy and hold strategies, not through day trading.

Options trading

Options trading is a bit like day trading in terms of risk but the trade lasts longer than a few hours. Essentially it is betting that a stock will go up or down in price and, if you are correct, you make money from it. If you are wrong, you lose money, and you can lose more than just your initial investment — sometimes much more. Options fall under a larger category called derivatives. In simple terms, it means the price depends on the price of something else. It's like buying a bunch of concert tickets in the hopes of reselling them for a profit... but the concert tickets' values are affected by how many shows the artist decides to put on (supply).

Options trading can be done by placing bets on stocks, bonds, ETFs or mutual funds. You're essentially putting a deposit down to buy or sell something in the future:

- When you make a call option, you are saying you want to buy shares at a certain price at a certain time. This isn't an obligation, however.

- When you make a put option you are saying you want to sell a certain number of shares at a certain time. This is not an obligation.

- You can 'long' or 'short' a stock, which is essentially betting that the stock price will rise or fall.

- You can also buy or sell other people's calls and puts. Buying them is 'longing' them and selling them is 'shorting' them.

It can all seem a bit confusing so let's go over a real example: GameStop in 2021.

When shorting goes wrong: GameStop

Remember how in chapter 5 I spoke about hedge funds making risky moves to try beat the market? Shorting stocks is one of them.

Some hedge funds saw GameStop as a company that was on the downfall, so they shorted it: essentially, they bet its stock price would drop. However, if the stock price went up they'd lose money.

Essentially, the hedge fund borrows (doesn't buy) a stock of GameStop, which at the time is around $10, from a broker. They sell it for $10 to an investor. They promise to buy back the stock from the investor at a certain time, regardless of its price at that time. So if the price of GameStop has dropped down to $7 by the time they have to buy it back, they buy that stock back from the investor for $7, making $3.

They borrowed a stock for free, charged someone $10 to buy it off them and then paid $7 for it back. The hedge fund has now profited $3. They then give the borrowed stock back to the broker. See figure 11.1 for an illustration of this.

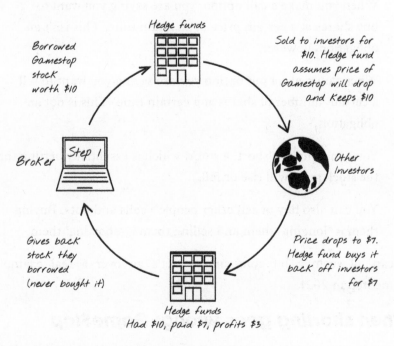

Figure 11.1: how hedge funds short stocks

The whole situation happened because retail investors (particularly those who were on Reddit's r/wallstreetbets forum) noticed that the hedge fund Melvin Capital was betting on the price dropping. They intentionally worked together to attempt to drive the price up, buying lots of GameStop stock. Due to much more demand than supply of the shares, the price rose quickly—from US$17.69 to US$325.

Melvin Capital then had to buy these shares back, now at a higher price—causing them to lose $6.8 billion in one month. The stock price has since come down considerably from its high, and those who bought at the peak of the frenzy have lost a lot of money. While it was a pretty one-off event, it's a great example of the downsides of shorting, the dangers of FOMO investing, and how speculative bubbles can form in the age of social media.

Forex trading

Forex (FX) is short for foreign exchange. It's very similar to day trading, but rather than trading stocks you are trading currencies. The price of currencies fluctuates throughout the day too. $1 USD may equal $1.37 AUD at 9 am but can be worth $1.39 by 8 pm.

The idea behind forex trading is that you buy into a currency when it is cheaper in price, and then when the currency goes up you sell it for a profit. Currencies are traded in pairs (e.g. USD/NZD).

For example, I could buy $100 USD when it's worth $150 NZD and then when $100 USD is worth $200 NZD I can sell it, making a $50 profit. It's not like gambling, however, as there are factors such as upcoming elections or trade deals that can indicate a change in currency price.

Forex trading is done on the foreign exchange market, also known as the currency market. This and the cryptocurrency exchange are the only two nonstop trading markets in the world. They don't stop at 4.30 pm and aren't closed on weekends.

The forex market is as volatile as the 'nice guy' who starts swearing at you when you reject his advances. But unlike with nice guys, you want volatility in the forex market. Factors such as interest rates, tourism and politics can affect the supply and demand of the currencies and thus cause them to fluctuate.

It's one of the most heavily traded markets in the world; banks use it, companies use it and retail investors can have access to it as well.

In the same way you can long and short stocks, you can long and short currencies, making money when the price of them increases or drops. The thing that makes forex trading interesting is leverage: you can use other people's money to make a lot of money very quickly, but in the same way you can lose that money just as fast.

Some companies also hedge through forex. For example, say you run a skincare company that is based in the US but you sell your products to New Zealand.

If a product costs you US$50 to make and you sell it for NZ$100, you'll run into the problem of the cost and sale price fluctuating and you may not have the stability you need to pay your employees.

If you short the NZD and buy USD, then the rise of the USD will offset any loss in profit from the sale of the skincare. And if the USD drops then you lose the short but the profit from the product itself makes up for it. As a result, you get to protect your company profits from the up and down of the market.

Investors in training know that with forex trading you're a small fish in a big pond, trading alongside major investment banks, full-time forex traders and hedge fund managers. In fact, retail investors only make up 5.5 per cent of forex traders, and they are more likely to lose money.

Cryptocurrency

Spanx, the shapewear brand, was founded by a young woman in her basement with a few thousand dollars. Now it's worth billions of dollars. Someone who doesn't understand shapewear may ask, why was it made and why is it so successful?

Cryptocurrency falls into the same category. It solves a problem, but the problem isn't so obvious.

'Normal' currency such as the USD or the British pound is at the mercy of governments and banks. Cryptocurrency was made to solve the issue of what would happen if governments or banks 'turned bad' and abused their power to control currency. It's hard to imagine that our governments and banks could lock all our bank accounts away from us forever, but I've lived through 2020 and it feels like crazier things have happened.

After the 2008 Global Financial Crisis, people wanted a currency that was completely decentralised from any government or institutions. An anonymous person going by the pseudonym Satoshi Nakamoto created the first cryptocurrency, Bitcoin, in January 2009. They released it with a document to explain how it worked, and then, like Cinderella, disappeared from the ball.

Except unlike Cinderella, Nakamoto has never been found.

Bitcoin

Bitcoin was created to be immune from government intervention or manipulation. It was created on blockchain technology which, in simple terms, is just like a long piece of paper that records and verifies every single Bitcoin transaction into blocks. Lots of computers around the world match this up and as a result everything is accounted for and verified.

Through the blockchain you can see where each Bitcoin has moved from. From my pocket to yours, to your neighbour's and then back to me. It's all tracked, and as a result it's almost impossible to counterfeit.

Cryptocurrencies aren't an investment like a stock of Coca-Cola or Apple—they're like currency, like the USD or rupees. It's basically forex trading.

When you invest in one Bitcoin, which was only worth US$1 in 2011, you make money when the value of the coin goes up. For example if you were lucky enough to purchase a Bitcoin for $1 in 2011, you could have sold it for US$1000 in 2013, making a profit of US$999. Or US$64 000 in 2021, making a profit of US$63 999.

The benefit of Bitcoin is that it is finite; there is a maximum number of Bitcoins. Some suggest that because of this it can be used as a hedge against inflation, in the same way gold or silver is.

Ethereum

Ethereum is the second-largest cryptocurrency by market capitalisation (the total number of coins multiplied by the value of each coin), founded by a 17-year-old Russian named Vitalik Buterin. Vitalik worked for a Bitcoin magazine (yes, a literal magazine about Bitcoin) where he would pitch ideas to his team on how to make improvements, which often got ignored. He ended up creating Ethereum in 2015. The system that it runs on is called Ethereum and the currency itself is called Ether.

Ethereum uses nodes, computer transactions and blockchaining, however, it has two main points of difference compared to Bitcoin.

The first is that the blockchain (list) is designed in such a way that transactions can only take place if all conditions are met. There's a thing called a smart contract that decides on the restrictions or rules.

The second is Decentralized Applications or dApps. Ethereum is basically flexible enough to allow other digital applications and programs to run on the Ethereum blockchain. In simple terms, Ethereum can be used to host gaming, social media and even financial services.

The downsides of crypto

One of the downsides of cryptocurrency is its real-world impact on climate change. The electricity used by Bitcoin alone is more than the electricity usage of entire countries such as UAE or the Netherlands. Bitcoin also causes over 30 kilotons of electronic waste (discarded computers, hardware etc.) every year. And this is just one cryptocurrency.

Another worrying point is the use of cryptocurrency by criminals. Due to the decentralised nature of cryptocurrency, it also can be used on the black market for illegal purchases that criminals don't want banks or governments to see. In 2020 alone, over $10 billion worth of cryptocurrency was used for illicit activities. This may result in an ethical dilemma for some investors, while others may not have an issue with it. Again, it's a personal choice.

Cryptocurrency alternative (alt) coins

Alt coins are the Wild West of the cryptocurrency world. See, anyone can make a cryptocurrency: there's Trump coin, garlic coin or coinYe (named after and officially sued by Kanye West).

There are more than 17 000 types of cryptocurrencies available, and this number continues to grow. Bitcoin and Ethereum make up 60 per cent of the total market of crypto, which leaves 40 per cent to the alt coins. After Bitcoin and Ethereum, some of the largest alt coins include XRP, Cardano, Litecoin, Dogecoin and Stellar.

Cryptocurrencies are already highly speculative investments, but at least Bitcoin (ticker: BTC) and Ethereum (ticker: ETH) have some real world use, such as hedging against inflation or being used as a blockchain to host new software and apps. Investors in training understand that the only kinds of investments that last are those with intrinsic value, which can be measured by their real-world applications.

Alternative coins, on the other hand, are even more speculative than ETH and BTC and have even less real-world value. They may prove useful on a smaller scale, but the rule of thumb is that, if it doesn't make sense to you, it probably doesn't make sense for a reason and you should consider minimising your position in it. That rule of not investing in what you don't understand can be transferred here.

Alt coin pump and dumps

One of the main issues with alt coins is that they can be the perfect vehicle for pump and dump schemes. Let me explain what I mean. Imagine I was a scammer. I create an alt coin with an attractive name like rainbowcoin (there probably is a rainbow coin out there already) and commission a cute picture of a rainbow to be the coin's icon. I can convince two to three really wealthy investors to drop some money into that coin.

When they do this the price of the coin rises, so I can take this graph and convince everyday investors that this is an 'up-and-coming coin'. With social media, my reach for this type of content has never been easier. I don't have to cold call people to try and prey on them (this concept is called boiler rooms); instead I can post content on social media and Reddit forums to create hype.

Retail investors would see the rise of the coin due to the original investors, and then pour more money into it, raising the price higher. It would continue and even more people would invest as they kept watching the price get higher and higher.

Then my original wealthy investors and I would sell all of our coins. This would make us, the scammers, extremely wealthy and leave the everyday investors holding essentially worthless cryptocurrency.

This is a modern pump and dump scheme, with the 'pump' caused by retail investors pouring in their money and the 'dump' achieved by scammers who dump their coins at a high price, take their gains and move on. (Pump and dump schemes were how Jordan Belfort, the real-world Wolf of Wall Street, made his money, but rather than pumping and dumping alt coins he used penny stocks, which can be thought of as alternative stocks from smaller, riskier, sometimes fake companies.)

Does cryptocurrency have a place in an investor's portfolio? An aggressive or growth investor may consider keeping cryptocurrency in their wallets, but investors in training must be wary of alternative cryptocurrencies and do thorough unbiased research on the creation of the cryptocurrency and its real-world usefulness.

A good rule of thumb is if you try to explain its use to a friend or family member and they don't really get it, it may not actually be all that useful.

NFTs

It's always easier explaining why something exists based off the problem it solves, so let's take that approach to NFTs.

It's very difficult to prove you own something digital, whether that be a piece of artwork, a video or even a tweet; it's easy for people to create counterfeits. It's very difficult to authenticate an item.

This is where NFTs come in. Short for nonfungible tokens, they are online tokens, like cryptocurrencies, that work using the blockchain. The similarities, however, stop there. Cryptocurrencies are fungible tokens, which means their value is the same. One Bitcoin in your pocket is worth the same as one Bitcoin in my pocket, in the same way that US$1 in your hand is worth the same as US$1 in my hand.

With nonfungible tokens, the value of one token is not the same as the value of another token. Each coin is unique and can't be replaced with something else. It's like a one-of-a-kind trading card.

The value of an NFT lies in the media attached to them. The most common NFTs are attached to art or music, but there is the potential to tokenise any real-world asset.

NFTs are a part of the Ethereum blockchain. It's like a digital fingerprint on an original item, and every time the ownership of that item gets transferred it can be recorded online on the blockchain, thus keeping the authenticity clear.

One of the benefits of NFTs is the real-world impact it has on artists. Artists can now mint (tokenise) their artwork on a network and bypass the galleries and companies that normally take a large percentage of the sale price. It should not be brushed over that NFTs have opened up a great way for artists in emerging countries to make a living for themselves. One of the benefits of NFTs to artists is that artists can continue to earn royalties even when the NFT is sold between customers; an artist continues to earn a 2 per cent cut from each future transaction.

These are what I like to refer to as aesthetic NFTs. They support artists but, besides this, they have no real-world implication. When you invest in an NFT project like this, you are basing your investing decision on the highly speculative idea that someone else will value the artwork to be worth more, and thus buy it off you for more, giving you a profit.

There are some useful NFTs out there. Useful NFTs are those that have some real-world implication and are probably the only NFTs worth your time if you're looking to make money from them.

Think of things like NFTs that can be used to purchase tickets for live events. They allow users to get verified and get opportunities for extras such as access to interviews, bonus music downloads and backstage passes.

Ticketmaster and the National Football League in the US recently decided to offer NFTs on special game passes, embracing the value the new technology can provide.

The issue with NFTs is that, unlike investing in companies where the intrinsic value is based off the company's products, management and revenue, the value of NFTs is entirely speculative. When an investment's value is solely based on what the next person is willing to pay for it, the power lies with the people. Making money from an NFT can be lucrative if you buy low and sell high, but it's a bit like a hot potato—you don't want to be the last person standing holding a US$10 000 NFT that no-one is interested in buying.

★★★

Spicy investments in general are much riskier than your average ETF, however, that doesn't mean they can't fit into an investor's portfolio—although they should be approached with caution. The main concern surrounding them is that, while some have intrinsic value, most are overhyped and can lose value very quickly. It's not unheard of to have an alt coin or NFT drop 70 per cent in value in a matter of hours, and for most investors in training, that's just a bit too much, too soon.

Options, forex and day trading, on the other hand, involve much more complicated materials and theories that investors in training should understand before diving in. The time involved compared to the outcome does not make sense for investors, beginner or experienced.

Actionable steps

1. Is there a spicy investment you'd be interested in? If so, which one and why?

2. Can you think of an example of a pump and dump scheme you've seen?

3. Quiz time: What are the two points that make Ethereum different to Bitcoin?

Investor profile

NAME: Jenny (pseudonym)

AGE: 26

JOB: Software engineer

SALARY: £36000

1. What does your investment portfolio look like?

£15000 invested, 1/4 in FTSE 100, 1/4 in UK infrastructure fund, 1/4 in S&P 500 and 1/4 in NASDAQ. I also have £1000 in crypto (mostly Bitcoin, some Ethereum and Solana too).

2. How much and how often do you invest?

I invest at least £800 a month, about a third of my net salary.

3. Why do you invest?

I invest so my future will have more options. I think one day I'd like to open my own café, which will require money. In case it doesn't do well as a business, I'd also like some back-up money.

4. Any tips for new investors?

Just give it a go! Start small and safe then you can always go bigger and riskier when you understand it a bit more!

Putting it all together

Investing in the stock market is a lot like getting into skincare. At the start you have no idea how it works. There's a lot of jargon that flies over your head. (What is 'slugging'?) You don't really grasp all the different strategies and regimes out there. (What order do you apply all these serums in?) You don't get how to integrate skincare routines into your life. (You want me to do *how* many steps before bed every night?) Then, as time goes on, you learn how it all operates and it starts to make sense.

You'll try a few products, make mistakes, find out what does and doesn't work for you, but eventually you get the hang of it. Then you'll start looking back and not understanding why it took you so long to start using sunscreen and retinol. (How could I have been so clueless?)

Investing in the stock market is no different. We all begin somewhere, often at zero. That doesn't mean that we have to stay there. Investing has never been more accessible; the only thing missing is the knowledge to bridge the gap.

Now let's take everything we've learned in the previous chapters in this book and put a plan together, step by step. If you haven't started yet, this will be perfect. If you have, this will still serve as a way to revitalise your portfolio and make sure you're on the right track. Skincare or investing, our routine can always be improved.

In this section, we'll get into the seven steps of getting started with investing:

Step #1: Unlearn those money mindsets
Step #2: Lay down those 5 bricks
Step #3: Work out your investing goals
Step #4: Work out your risk profile
Step #5: Work out your asset allocation
Step #6: Choose where to invest
Step #7: Buy your shares

And then we'll wrap it up with the five most common mistakes of beginner investors and how to avoid them. Let's go!

Step #1: Unlearn those money mindsets

The mindset of someone who is privileged is completely different to the mindset of someone who is just trying to survive. If you are in the 'survive' category, this is going to be a much bigger uphill battle. You may be struggling with money or financial abuse trauma, or have neurodivergent tendencies—there can be a range of factors that affect how you interact with money. Our mind and how we are able to process things plays a huge impact on our ability to grow our wealth. For some of us it may just be a case of unlearning poor money habits we learnt from our parents, while for others it's much deeper.

If that is the case, you're dealing with a different set of hurdles and it may be worth exploring this further with therapy or professional help. I've heard stories of people saying budgeting and saving was a never-ending nightmare for them until they went to therapy and uncovered much deeper-rooted reasons for their behaviour.

The next step is unlearning the idea that we are just bad with money. An investor in training has a growth mindset; they understand that they are a sponge and are picking up information and refining their investing style.

Money doesn't have to be associated with greed. Money just makes a greedy person greedier.

Instead, money should be viewed as a key that unlocks your ability to do more of what you love, and do it on your own time.

Journaling is usually one of the best ways to unlearn and understand money mindsets. A few journal prompts to ask yourself include:

- What would I do if I had 40 extra hours a week? Would I use them to work more? If not, where would I prefer to allocate my time, and why?

- Why do I think I'm unable to reach my financial goals? What barriers are in my way and are they 100 per cent impossible to overcome?

- How was money introduced to me as a child? Was I taught to fear it or embrace it?

- Did I have any role models who displayed good money behaviour? Is there someone I look up to now who displays those behaviours? Could I invite them out for a coffee to chat about this?

Step #2: Lay down those 5 bricks

It doesn't feel like the most glamorous way to start building wealth, but looking back and understanding where our money is coming from and where it's going is essential.

We cover the 5 bricks in chapter 3, and they're a good way to make sure you're not building your investments on shaky ground.

This is the hardest step for investors in training, as you'll see investing itself isn't so difficult; it's facing your money and potentially your financial flaws that we don't like. It's the equivalent of buying those super magnified bathroom mirrors that show you the blackheads you didn't know you had. We'd all prefer to not know.

But in order to become an investor, we need to know. Block out time in your calendar to sit down for two hours this week, or one hour over two weeks if you're time poor, to put all 5 bricks in place, so your investment portfolio has a solid foundation.

Journal prompt for step 2:

- Go to page 48 and complete the 5 steps listed there to establish your financial foundation.

Step #3: Work out your investing goals

We'd all love an extra $100000, but knowing why you want to grow your money puts more intention behind it. More intention leads to more action. Investors in training also know having a goal in mind prevents them from treating their investment portfolio like an extra bank account, pulling out money when they need it—that's what an emergency fund is for.

Take a moment to put this book down and really think about why you want to grow your wealth. 'I want more money' is a surface-level reason. It's not the real reason. What would more money mean to you?

See the journal prompts at the end of this section for specific questions to consider.

Your investing goals should also have a time frame. Investors in training don't want to save up for a home deposit 'one day'. The want to have $X in Y years.

Knowing how long you want to invest for also provides you with the path you need to take in terms of risk and asset allocation.

Whether you're investing for the

- short term (1–3 years)

- medium term (3–10 years)

- long term (10-plus years)

your investing approach will be different.

These are deep, thought-provoking and maybe sightly intrusive questions. Consider the following journal questions:

- Do you want to invest to retire early so that you can travel, because you feel like you only have a finite time on this earth and travelling young is very important to you?

- Do you want to invest to retire early, so you can spend more time with your family?

- Do you want to invest to buy a home because the security of owning the roof over your head means a lot to you?

- Do you want to invest so that you can stand on your own two feet because you value being independent from a partner or your parents?

Step #4: Work out your risk profile

In the spirit of my generation, which spent too much time taking BuzzFeed quizzes during lectures, let's work out your risk tolerance with a quiz.

1. You can withdraw your money from your investment at any time. When would you likely want to withdraw?

   (A)   0–3 years

   (B)   4–10 years

   (C)   10-plus years

2. What would help you sleep easier at night?

   (A)   having my money on a stable but low rate of return, rather than risking losing my money

   (B)   accepting some short-term fluctuations with the chance of slightly higher returns

   (C)   knowing that I have higher odds of maximising my returns, but also a greater chance of losing money

3. What do you want your investments to do for you?

   (A)   provide me a steady cash flow right now to supplement my income

   (B)   grow over time, with some cash flow in the present as well

   (C)   grow over time, I'm not interested in touching that money for anything soon

4. You work for a FAANG company (Facebook, Apple, Amazon, Netflix or Google) and your boss is going to pay a year-end

bonus. You have a choice between $800 cash or $1000 in company stock, but you can't sell the stock for at least 12 months, and in that time the stock price could go up or down. What do you do?

(A) take the cash

(B) ask for 50 per cent cash, 50 per cent company stock

(C) take the company stock

5. This graph (figure A) shows the results for three funds over a one-year period. The top shows potential returns while the bottom shows potential loss. Which fund would you choose?

(A) Fund A: total 4 per cent gain

(B) Fund B: total 5 per cent gain

(C) Fund C: total 10 per cent gain

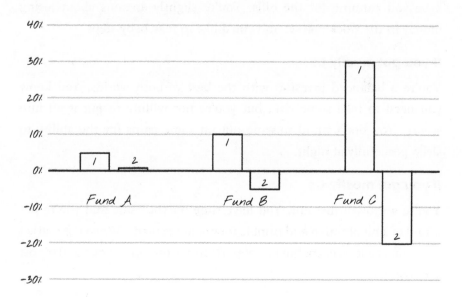

Figure A: three funds over one year

6. When I hear 'risk' related to investing:

    (A) I worry about losing my hard-earned money

    (B) I understand it's a normal part of investing

    (C) I see it as an opportunity for better returns

7. I feel that money is

    (A) scarce

    (B) something that I can leverage

    (C) something that can come in abundance

Answers

If you got mostly As

You're more likely to be a conservative investor. You'll take on some risk, but the idea of anything more than pretty minimal risk levels will have you running for the hills. You're slightly anxious about losing money in the stock market and you'd like to take baby steps.

If you got mostly Bs

You're a balanced investor, with the best of both worlds. You know you need to take some risk, but you're not willing to put it all into stocks. You don't mind missing out on some gains for the ability to sleep peacefully at night.

If you got mostly Cs

You're a growth investor. You have time on your side and you're not afraid of a bit of rough and tumble for greater returns. When the market dips you see it as extra buying opportunities on top of your dollar cost averaging.

If you got mostly Cs but you feel like you'd take on as much risk as possible with zero regret, you may fall into an aggressive portfolio.

Step #5: Work out your asset allocation

Based on your risk profile as a conservative, balanced or growth investor in training, you can now design your investing portfolio allocations. This is called asset allocation and is quite an empowering step to growing your investment profile. You're basically deciding how much money you want to put towards different investments. See table A.

Table A: asset allocation

Risk profile	Cash/fixed income	Bonds	Stocks/ ETFs	Speculative investments
Conservative	20 per cent	50 per cent	30 per cent	0 per cent
Balanced	10 per cent	40 per cent	48–50 per cent	0–2 per cent
Growth	0–5 per cent	10 per cent	80 per cent	0–5 per cent
Aggressive	0–5 per cent	0–5 per cent	90 per cent	0–10 per cent

The beauty of investing is that you can always change your asset allocation; you don't have to make your bed and lie in it. Investors in training know they can be dynamic and change their investing style to suit their needs. Most people may begin as an aggressive investor in their early twenties and thirties (if they're not trying to invest for a house deposit) and over the years slowly move to more conservative styles. By the time you're close to needing to pull your money out, you should be in a more conservative fund. After all, if you are about to pull out $100 000, you don't want that to drop 5 per cent the day before you need that cash.

So, to get the maximum gains should you take on the maximum risk possible? Surprisingly, no.

Figure B (overleaf) shows the risk versus return tradeoff. It's important to note: higher risk eventually plateaus your return, and you may be taking on more risk for the return on investment that you're after. It's a bit like running on a treadmill for 30 minutes every day. For a while, the more days you do it, the fitter you get, but after a while running for 30 minutes will plateau your progress, and you'll need to add other forms of exercise into the mix.

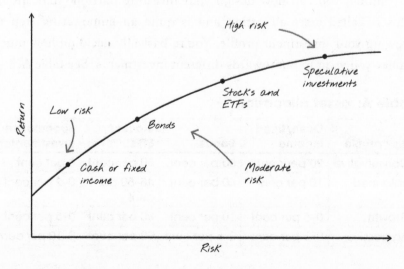

Figure B: risk versus return

You also need to decide if you are going to invest in individual stocks or if you'd take the lazy investor strategy. Investors in training tend to keep 90 per cent of their portfolio in the strategy they have signed themselves up for, but can keep a small percentage of their portfolio for individual stocks, crypto and/or NFTs.

An investment portfolio can also be divided up and include a portion of:

- **a growth portfolio** where the investor in training is trying to maximise their capital gains

- **a value portfolio** where they are trying to invest based off fundamental analysis

- **a dividend-heavy portfolio** where they are trying to live off their income

- **an active profile** where they're trying to use technical analysis to find winning day trading stocks based off movements.

Once the basics are covered, investors in training may want to add in further alternative investments such as REITs or commodities. They may also decide to invest in ETFs or companies that reflect their ethical and impact values.

Step #6: Choose where to invest

Choosing where to invest is one of the biggest barriers investors face. It can be so overwhelming it puts many investors off from being there in the first place, and it's a huge source of analysis paralysis.

There's a number of ways to invest, and we'll go through them all. But in short, one of the easiest and most cost effective ways to invest is through an online investing broker.

Online brokers

A broker used to be a person you'd call up to buy your investments from. They were the middleman, and sometimes they'd add a hint of pressure into their sales pitch, but thankfully we've moved away from that.

The most common type of online investing broker is a DIY one (think Robinhood). It's a website or app that acts as the communication portal between you and the stock exchange that you are interested in.

In every country there are online investing brokers. So how do you decide which one to go for? There are a few questions investors in training use to vet them.

1. *What exchanges and countries do they invest in?* For example, one broker in your country may be limited to the exchange in your

country (e.g. just the NZX in New Zealand), while another broker will offer that plus the exchanges in the US.

2. *How easy is it to navigate the user interface?* It's like vetting a gym before starting a membership. Is it simple, well-lit and friendly or is it filled with gym rats who could probably snap you in half? If you don't feel comfortable, you're less likely to go back. In the beginning, having a brokerage site that you enjoy and that is easy to navigate can make all the difference.

3. *What fees are involved?* There are a number of fees that you may have to pay when you invest.

- **transaction fees:** the fee to buy a stock, e.g. $3 for every transaction; some brokerages have 'fee free' trading, but hike up fees in other areas

- **expense ratios:** if you buy a fund, they'll have a percentage fee that the fund takes; this can range from 0.02 per cent up to 1 to 2 per cent if they're actively managed (it's important to note that a broker doesn't charge this, the fund does!)

- **front- and back-end fees:** fees the brokerage takes to help set up and close down your account

- **management fees:** some brokerages charge these

- **annual fees:** some brokerages charge you a membership to use their platform

- **fx fees:** if you're investing in the US share market but you need to convert your British pounds first (for example), brokerages usually charge a fee for this conversion, usually 0.2 to 1 per cent.

Fees matter but it ultimately depends on what you're going to invest in and how often you're going to invest. For example, someone investing $50 a month is better off with a percentage-based fee than investing with a brokerage that takes a $5 cut every time.

However, someone else who invests $500 a month might be better off with the $5 fee, as the percentage fee is now higher than $5.

4. *How secure is the brokerage?* When you invest there is a risk that if your brokerage goes down, your investments can go down with them. (Though this is rare.) There are some long-term brokers who may be better suited to you if this risk is important to you. Make sure to check what:

- levels of security they offer

- their insurance policy is (are they promising to give you your money back if they go under?)

- their fraud policies are.

Investors in training know to stay away from startup investment brokers that haven't been around very long. Often these brokers try to grow quickly and sell off their company. Their end goal may not always be to keep their customers happy.

5. *Can you have your funds in your name?* Some brokers will put the shares you own under your name, while others will put them under their name for ease of management. You still get to buy, sell and withdraw them regardless, so this isn't important to many investors. However some investors like the ability to have full voting rights on the shares they own, and it's easier to move shares around different brokers if they own them, so it's important to check if this is the case.

Investment company platforms

You can invest in mutual funds directly with the companies that own them. This may save you on fees, and if you are investing with a higher amount (e.g. $1000 a month) then you don't need to worry about fractional shares and can invest in an index fund directly.

An example of this would be investing through Vanguard's website into their funds. The downside of doing this, however, is that these platforms will push their own products more than any other investment option available, as they have incentive to do so. And some will not offer other investments at all.

Financial planners/advisers

You can invest with a financial adviser. They are professionals who are regulated by their governing bodies to provide you investing advice suited to your needs. This book may not know the ins and outs of your circumstances, your beliefs, values and financial background, but an adviser will be able to guide you through the process.

It is not uncommon for an investor who usually DIYs their portfolio to seek an adviser if they have recently received an inheritance or a large bonus and are unsure how to navigate their money to reach their goals faster.

There are two fee payment mechanisms for financial advice. A fee-based method where you pay a fee and a built-in commission to the investment product. This can vary where you live. For example, in Australia, no financial adviser, by law, can receive a built-in commission (and no products offer this) and most charge a fee for investment advice. Whereas in the United States, there are both options available to consumers. The key here is to understand that professionals do not work for free and it's totally okay to ask how any financial professional is remunerated before you engage them. If you are worried about biased opinions, you can always seek a fee-based professional adviser.

Robo-advisers

I'm inclined to say robo-advisers are the new kid on the block but 2008 wasn't a few years ago anymore. Robo-advisers act like artificially intelligent financial advisers. They ask you some questions to gain an idea of what kind of investor you are, and invest on your behalf by setting up an investment portfolio customised to you.

Robo-advisers are good as a set-and-forget option and usually charge a flat fee of around 0.2 to 0.8 per cent per fund, and they can also provide assistance if needed.

The issue with robo-advisers is that if you know what you want to invest in, or you suddenly want to change your investments, you possibly have less control over this decision because your portfolio has been chosen for you. You can't suddenly go buy that GameStop share with a robo-adviser.

Step #7: Buy your shares

Now that you've decided what you want to invest in and with which online broker, it's time to begin.

1. First, create an online profile with the broker of your choice in your country. They usually require some ID so make sure to have that close by.

2. Deposit money into your account. How much should you start with? Generally, $100–500 is a good place for many investors in training. You may have to wait a couple days for this money to show up and you may incur a foreign exchange fee.

3. Search for the funds you are after by their ticker name. For example, Apple is 'APPL' or the Vanguard S&P 500 ETF is 'VOO' (or VVI, depending on where you live). Once you click on the share, you can see the market movement of the share over the last day, week, month or years.

4. You can then choose how much money you want to put into the funds based off the asset allocation that you decided on earlier. With fractional shares it doesn't matter if a fund is $1000 a share, you can still put in $100 or even technically $1. It's important to note that if you are investing in an overseas fund or share, the overseas exchange may not be open at the same time you're looking to invest due to time zone differences. So you can buy it today but your money will be held by the brokerage and won't actually buy your investment until the market is open. This can sometimes mean you expect to buy a fund for $200 on Friday, but by Monday morning you see you actually bought the fund for $204 as the price changed.

5. When you buy a stock or fund, you'll see three options to buy your stock:
   i. **Market order:** paying whatever price the brokerage can get you. If you buy it and the stock is $100 but by the time the order goes through it goes up to $101, you pay $101.
   ii. **Limit buy order:** this instructs your broker to buy stock at a certain price (e.g. if the stock is worth $50 but you won't buy it until it's down to $45, you can set a limit where it is automatically bought for you when the price drops).
   iii. **Stop buy order:** like a limit buy order, but it automatically buys it for you if the price rises. (Why would someone do this? To protect against the potentially unlimited losses of an uncovered short position—this tool is more for traders than long-term investors.)

6. You can also set up your investments into the autoinvest category, allowing you to make these investments every fortnight or month, taking the money from your online account that you set up under your bank account when you set up your 5 bricks. So your income will go into your online bank account until it reaches a certain number (e.g. $500), then at the appointed time it will get autoinvested.

Avoid these 5 beginner investor mistakes

A wise person learns from their mistakes; a wiser person learns from the mistakes of others. Here are five of the most common mistakes investors in training make, so you can avoid them before you begin.

Not rebalancing your portfolio

Remember how we worked so hard to set up our portfolios, say 20 per cent bonds and 80 per cent funds? At the end of the year you'll notice your funds will grow faster than your bonds, and you might see the percentages have shifted to 10 per cent bonds and 90 per cent stocks. This is called portfolio drift and it puts you in a riskier position. You need to rebalance your portfolio by either selling some of your stock to buy bonds, or adding in more bonds. You only need to do this if your portfolio has shifted 5 per cent off its mark, however, so if you moved from 20/80 per cent bonds and stocks to 17/83 per cent bonds and stock, you don't need to rebalance.

Assuming all IPOs make retail investors profits

IPOs used to be a great time to invest in up-and-coming companies. They're cheaper, after all: when Apple IPO'd it was trading for about US$22 a share. However, in more recent times, IPOs can fall victim to FOMO investing, where you may see a large spike in the stock in the first few days, followed by a large drop. For example, when Oatly, an oat milk company, went public, many investors thought due to its great ESG rating it would perform well in the long term (see figure C, overleaf).

However, once the music stopped, investors realised that potential growth for oat-based alternative milk was not as large as had been originally proclaimed, and there was rising competition (there's more than one oat milk brand out there, and there is more than one milk alternative available).

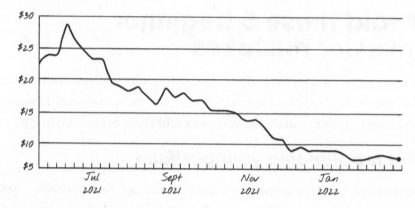

Figure C: Oatly's IPO
Source: Courtesy of Nasdaq

In November 2021, Oatly had a quality issue causing it to throw out some products. They also ran into production shortages due to technical issues — and if that wasn't enough, driver shortages delayed the delivery of the product into stores. Talk about a bad start.

A rule of thumb is to never invest in an IPO solely based off public attention or hype. (Oatly was branded as 'Oprah-backed' due to the support of the widely popular talk show host, among an array of high-profile figures, such as Natalie Portman and Jay Z.)

Was Oatly just a bad...oat?

Not really. A 2018 report by Dimensional Fund Advisors looked at the performance of over 6000 US IPOs from 1991 to 2018, and found that in their first year they tended to underperform their industry's benchmarks. They weren't even average.

Setting unrealistic expectations

Stock market investing can make you a millionaire, but investors in training know that stock market investing is not going to make you a millionaire overnight. Or even in a few years. There are always headlines of how people made gains in the market — heck, I was one of them — but it's circumstantial and often requires a large amount of capital to create those gains, along with a sprinkle of luck (like investing at the bottom of a COVID-19 crash without knowing it was the bottom).

The market returns that magical 7 to 10 per cent on average, but this means some years it may return 34 per cent (e.g. in 1995) and another year −38 per cent (e.g. in 2008). It's about setting realistic expectations.

Not taking into account tax obligations

Tax is often an overlooked part of investing. Investors in training don't want to be surprised with a tax bill they weren't expecting after their first year of investing.

Tax laws will vary country by country, but most countries treat stocks like real estate. If your country has a capital gains tax on property, it likely has capital gains on shares. Once you sell your share, you need to pay capital gains tax on the profit you've made as well. This is often done at the end of the financial year along with your income tax filings.

Your dividends are also taxed, and this is usually done in accordance with your tax bracket. If you're a lower income earner, your dividend tax will be lower than if you are in a higher tax bracket.

Some countries offer tax breaks or credits to investors, so it is always advised to seek a tax professional for any country-specific questions you may have.

Not normalising investing conversations

I believe that once we begin taking control and growing our money, we should make it a habit to involve and share this knowledge with our friends and family. We talk about our bowel movements (or is that just me?) but shy away from the conversations about growing wealth and financial freedom.

Having a circle of friends who are open to learning and growing together is a powerful way to move ahead together. Every single person has something to teach us. Setting up a monthly brunch with your friends to discuss and go over your investments is an activity that is starting to become more normalised, and benefits everyone involved.

Graduations & ladders

And that's it! You've just graduated as an investor in training, with your own investing portfolio built out of tried-and-tested strategies and research-backed knowledge.

A common theme among investors in training is that, when they start to understand these concepts and feel ready to begin investing, they feel a ping of regret and sadness that they weren't taught this sooner.

But I believe it's unfair to be so harsh on our past selves, especially given the history women and minorities have had with investing. Not all of us had the privilege of generational wealth. However, we can now be the change makers in our families and set ourselves and our future generations up for success.

Investing isn't as difficult as it's made out to be, and I hope through this book you've been able to realise, chapter by chapter, how simple most of these concepts are when they're not doused in complicated terminology. Investing can and should be for everyone, but especially for those of us who have been left out of the conversation for too long.

Before I leave you, I want to ask one favour. A promise my father asked me to make; I am now asking you.

Investing isn't just a sole-person activity. We invest for our communities and our families. Growing wealth doesn't just benefit us; it benefits our society as a whole. When we uplift ourselves we inspire our friends, our siblings, our nieces and nephews and even those we never thought we would. We inspire future generations by being the role models they deserve.

The information in this book isn't just to benefit you, but to help those around you as well. Like my father told me, when you reach those financial goals you are after—because you will—do not forget to look back at how far you have come and make sure you help others climb up the ladder too.

There is enough space for us all.

Can't get enough?

Join our Investing Masterclass, taken by over 3000 students across 60 countries.

The Girls That Invest Investing Masterclass is a comprehensive six-week step-by-step educational roadmap to help you go from a complete beginner to a confident and knowledgeable investor, from anywhere in the world. Created by the world's largest investing podcast for women.

Visit **girlsthatinvest.com** to find out more.

Here's what some of our students have to say:

'The knowledge in this course is incredible. I thought I knew a decent amount before starting this but the breadth of knowledge that this provides goes beyond the basic investor. Module 8-10 just really took my understanding to the next level!'

'I loved Sim's laid back delivery of the content. It made it feel so reassuring that its actually all quite simple once you have a basic understanding.'

'I have learnt soo much from this masterclass. I was afraid at first but feel I am taking the necessary steps for future me! I feel more confident than ever to start this journey. Thank you!'

Index